MOVING
MOUNTAINS

MOVING MOUNTAINS

How to See the Sick Healed and Captives Set Free

RICHIE LEWIS

© Copyright 2016 – Richie Lewis

All rights reserved. This book is protected by the copyright laws of the United States of America. This book may not be copied or reprinted for commercial gain or profit. The use of short quotations or occasional page copying for personal or group study is permitted and encouraged. Permission will be granted upon request. Unless otherwise identified, Scripture is taken from the New King James Version®. Copyright © 1982 by Thomas Nelson. Used by permission. All rights reserved. Scripture quotations marked (NLT) are taken from the Holy Bible, New Living Translation, copyright © 1996, 2004, 2007 by Tyndale House Foundation. Used by permission of Tyndale House Publishers, Inc., Carol Stream, Illinois 60188. All rights reserved. Scriptures quoted from the International Children's Bible®, copyright ©1986, 1988, 1999, 2015 by Tommy Nelson. Used by permission. Scripture quotations marked ASV are from the American Standard Version, now in the public domain and available at: BibleGateway.com. Emphasis within scripture is author's own.

Paginated text and cover design by: Karen Webb

ISBN: 978-1533496195

For Worldwide Distribution, Printed in the U.S.A.

Dedication

This book is dedicated to Jesus Christ. When I was at my lowest point, You came in and turned my life around. I owe You everything.

From the moment You entered my life, Your amazing goodness filled my heart with an unquenchable passion to see other people enter into a relationship with You. Life with You has been the greatest adventure. There is nothing more exhilarating than being a co-laborer with You, stepping out and seeing lives transformed.

What an amazing privilege it is to have a relationship with The Creator of all things. Words could never adequately express how my heart feels towards You!

Acknowledgements

A special thanks to my father-in-law Dave Hess, and brother-in-law Brandon Hess, for encouraging me to write this book. Without your encouragement this book would have never been written. Thank you Dave, for your help in editing this book!

To my mother and father, Rich and Valerie Lewis: You are the best parents I could have asked for! I am convinced that I am saved today because of your prayers during my difficult teenage years.

To my wife, Bethany Lewis and son Micah Lewis: You are wonderful gifts from God. I can't imagine life without you. Thank you for all your love and support.

Endorsements

This life changing book will help shape the destiny of believers for generations to come. It is a clear, easy to read, insightful, liberating, and empowering revelation of Scriptural truth! The reader of this book will be soundly equipped to do the "greater works" Jesus spoke of in John 14:12. If you have a desire see the sick healed and captives set free this book is a must read!

Tony Sweet
Senior Pastor, Kingdom Life Ministries
Harrisburg, Pennsylvania

This book is a "Must Read" for anyone with a desire to walk out their faith by healing the sick, binding up the broken hearted, and setting the captives free. It reveals some incredible truths and exposes some deeply ingrained lies of the enemy. Richie is an anointed evangelist, and teacher who has come into his calling. I have been walking with him in his evangelistic ministry, Sent Ones, in Harrisburg, Pennsylvania for the past 5 years. I have personally seen and been part of many of the things he describes in his book.

His revelation, relative to commanding healing has been a "game changer" in my personal outreach ministry. Richie has done a phenomenal job in articulating the concepts and ideas that the Holy Spirit has taught him, and has provided the scriptural references that validate his teachings. I would highly recommend this book for any believer who wants to see results from their faith in action and would encourage members of the five-fold ministry to be actively teaching these truths.

Pastor Scott Heiland
Presiding Elder
City of Refuge Evangelism (CORE)

Table of Contents

Foreword 13

CHAPTER ONE
My Story 17

CHAPTER TWO
Testimonies 25

CHAPTER THREE
Speaking to Your Mountain 37

CHAPTER FOUR
The Authority EVERY Believer Has 51

CHAPTER FIVE
Healing and Atonement 65

CHAPTER SIX
Is it Gods Will for
Everyone to Be Healed? 77

CHAPTER SEVEN
The Role of the Believer vs.
The Role of the 5-Fold Minister 93

CHAPTER EIGHT
Seeing through the Eyes of Christ 105

CHAPTER NINE
Paul's Thorn in the Flesh 113

CHAPTER TEN
Do You Need Faith to be Healed? 125

CHAPTER ELEVEN
Being Led by the Spirit 133

Appendix A
Step by Step Instructions
on How to Minister Healing 143

Appendix B
Resources. 147

Appendix C
Information about Sent Ones. 149

About the Author 151

Foreword

God has always wanted to heal us!

Since the day of Adam's rebellion in the Garden of Eden—and the deadly impact sin had on our spirits, our souls, and our bodies—God has been intent on restoring us!

His promise to send His Son, Jesus, is filled with His desire to heal us:

> "*Do not fear. Your God will come…He will come to save you. The eyes of the blind will be opened and the ears of the deaf unstopped. The lame will leap like a deer, and the mute tongue will shout for joy!*" (Isaiah 35:3-6 [My paraphrase]).

In fact, in the Talmud (written by the religious leaders 500 years before the birth of Jesus), they said:

> "When the Messiah comes, He will sit among the poor and the suffering sick. He will be a Wounded Healer—One who will first carry our sicknesses in order to bring us healing" (Sanhedrin 98a).[1]

Jesus, our Healer, fully experienced our need for Him. He loves us! He cares about everything that touches us! Isaiah the prophet described His deep compassion this way:

> "He was despised and rejected by men, a man of sorrows; and fully acquainted with grief" (Isaiah 53:3 [My paraphrase]).

Isaiah then added these hope-filled promises, guarantees of Jesus' power to heal and restore us in every area of our lives:

> "Surely, He took up our infirmities (disease, sickness) and carried our sorrows (debilitating grief; depression)...He was pierced for our transgressions (actual sins) and He was crushed for our iniquities ("why" we sin; root cause—selfishness). The punishment that brought us peace (joy; well-being) was upon Him, and by His wounds we are healed (rapha—complete healing throughout)" (Isaiah 53:4-5 [My paraphrase]).

No single verse describes Jesus' amazing ministry quite like this:

"God anointed Jesus of Nazareth with the Holy Spirit and power, and how he went around doing good and healing all who were under the power of the devil, because God was with him" (Acts 10:38, NIV).

He is still healing people today!

The book you hold in your hand reflects the deep passion of its author. Richie Lewis not only believes Jesus can heal—he walks in faith with Jesus and participates with Him as He heals people.

Today.

Continually.

Our family met Richie a number of years ago through our daughter, Bethany, introducing him as a "friend" from Elim Bible College in Lima, New York. Within a short period of time, we watched her fall in love with this "friend." It didn't take long for us to love Richie, too.

As a father-in-law, I consider Richie my "son," and he is a son I am very proud of! He is a man of integrity and strong conviction. The stories you will read are absolutely true, experienced by a man who trusts Jesus implicitly and follows Him whole-heartedly. Your heart will be stirred. Your faith will be strengthened. And your life will be challenged to join a growing community of Jesus-followers who love people and see them healed!

Dave Hess
Senior Pastor, Christ Community Church
Camp Hill, Pennsylvania
Author of: *Hope Beyond Reason*
and *Hope Beyond Disappointment*

— END NOTE —

1. James, Drummond, *The Jewish Messiah a Critical History of the Messianic Idea Among the Jews from the Rise of the Maccabees to the Closing of the Talmud* (Longmanns, Green, 1877), page 281.

chapter one

My Story

I have always believed God could heal people and that He could even use me to heal the sick. Unfortunately, my experience had always contradicted my beliefs—that is—until September 18, 2010.

I was born again in mid-August 1999—one month shy of my 22nd birthday. From day one, I have been on fire for God, and have had an unquenchable passion to share the good news with others. There was something inside of me that felt compelled to tell others what Jesus had done for me. I told everyone I could—family members, friends, co-workers, and even random strangers about Jesus. Sharing the gospel was (and still is) my all-consuming passion. As a result I've had the amazing privilege of leading many people to the Lord.

During my first 11 years, after being saved, I preached the gospel to thousands of people. Many times, while talking to someone, they would ask me to pray for an illness or injury. Over those first eleven years, I prayed for hundreds of people to be healed. I can honestly say that I never saw one person healed. This sounds almost humorous, being a born again Christian, believing in the healing power of Christ, yet never experiencing it. Through all those years I didn't give up, but kept asking Him through prayer, for deliverance and healing for people with no physical results.

All that changed on Saturday, September 18, 2010. This day (The Day of Atonement that year.), was a day that I will never forget. While in Bible school, I developed a passion for inner city, street evangelism. For four years I led groups of Bible school students to minister on the streets of Rochester, New York. When I got married, I moved to Harrisburg, Pennsylvania. In 2008, I began doing street evangelism with a small group from my church in Harrisburg. We would go out once or twice a month on a Saturday afternoon. That Saturday (September 18, 2010) we were scheduled to go out and minister to people on the street.

The night before, my wife Bethany and our 18-month-old son Micah stayed the night at her parent's house because they were going to help her parents with a yard sale. Those of you with young children understand what it's like to be sleep deprived. I hadn't gotten much sleep over the past 18 months and was excited to have the house to myself for one night. My normal routine each morning was to go for a prayer walk around my neighborhood, then spend some time reading my Bible.

Being the first chance I've had to sleep in for a year and a half, I took full advantage of it. I slept until I couldn't sleep any more. By the time I woke up, I had just enough time to take a shower, get dressed, and get something to eat before I had to meet the team in the city. I still wanted to connect with God before going out. Instead of going for a prayer walk and reading my Bible, I turned on some worship music to listen to as I got ready.

While worshiping, I sensed the presence of God all over me. It felt like I was in the midst of a good worship service at church. I could feel His presence and streams of tears began rolling down my face. (You know how it is when you really enter into God's presence.) But something was different this time. His presence kept getting stronger. I have felt the presence of God countless times in my life, but I have only felt it this strong one other time. In my senior year in Bible school a revival broke out on campus — the manifest presence of God was overpowering—just as it was this day.

His presence was so strong that it felt like a thousand pounds were on my shoulders. I was literally crushed, face down, on the hardwood floor of our dining room. When I first entered His presence, I had a few streams of tears gently flowing down the sides my face. Now, I was full-fledged wailing. Sobbing uncontrollably with snot and tears everywhere (I know, not a pretty sight!), I felt heat come over me, from the top of my head to the bottom of my feet. It was so hot that I began to sweat. I was shaking violently, my entire body convulsing—even if I wanted to, I couldn't control it. I couldn't stand up. I was flat on my face before God.

Then, the Lord spoke to me in a loud, clear voice saying, "When you minister healing to people today, I don't want you to pray for them."

This took me off guard. I remember asking Him, "How will they get healed if I don't pray for them?"

The Lord continued, and said, "When people ask you to pray for some kind of illness or injury instead of praying over them I want you to *declare* healing over them."

Then the Lord spoke a Scripture to me, "By My stripes they are healed." This is from Isaiah 53:5 which says:

> "But He was wounded for our transgressions, He was bruised for our iniquities; The chastisement for our peace was upon Him, And by His stripes we are healed."

He went on to say, "Two thousand years ago when I went to the cross, I paid the price for your sin. Before I went to the cross, I was whipped and beaten and paid the price for physical healing. I've *already* done my part. My part is finished. So don't pray and ask Me to do something I have *already* done! Instead, *declare* what I have done over them!"

Here's an example of what the Lord was saying. If I was praying for a person with a broken arm, in the past I would pray something like this:

> *"Jesus would you please heal this person's broken arm?"*

I prayed this way hundred's of times and nothing instant or miraculous ever happened. What God was telling me to do was to *declare healing instead of pray for healing*. One of my favorite teachers, Curry Blake, says it like this:

> "We are supposed to talk to the sickness about God, not talk to God about the sickness."[1]

In other words, when praying for someone with a broken arm I should have been saying something like this:

> *"In the name of Jesus, arm be healed."*

Please understand, this is not a formula. It's less about the words you speak, and more about the intent of your heart. But there are basic principles involved, such as declaring, instead of praying. Using the authority God has given you, instead of begging God to heal. You don't have to get the words "just perfect."

I remember being on the floor sobbing, and weeping in the heavy, weighty presence of God and thinking, "Okay God, I'll be glad to do what you are asking me to do. But right now I physically can't get up off the ground and I'm supposed to leave for the outreach in a few minutes!"

The moment I had that thought, He lifted just enough of His presence off of me so I could get up. His presence was still weighty—I was still sobbing and shaking like crazy—but I could stand to my feet. I remember driving to the outreach that day. My hands shook so much that it affected how I drove. I remember the entire way there my car swerved back and forth. I still can't believe I didn't have an accident or get pulled over for "drunk" driving. God surely saw me safely to my destination that day. (For the next 24 hours I felt the overwhelming presence of God. I succumbed to bouts of crying and shaking. I continued to feel heat throughout my body—from head to toe. None of this lifted until after church on Sunday.)

When I got to the outreach I told the team about my experience that morning. I encouraged them to declare healing over people, instead of praying and asking God to heal them. That very day, we saw nine different people healed instantly of various physical issues.

— END NOTE —

1. http://www.divinerevelations.info/documents/healing/jgl/jgl_ministries.htm (Accessed April 28, 2016.)

chapter two

Testimonies

BACK PAIN HEALED

I will never forget the first person I saw instantly healed—this was on Vernon Street in Harrisburg. I approached a man who seemed to be in a lot of pain.

While speaking with him, he said, "I have some severe back issues. I can barely bend down and touch my knees."

I replied, "Can I pray for you?"

He said, "Yes!"

As I declared healing over him, tears started rolling down his face. I asked "What do you feel?"

He said, "The pain...all the pain is gone."

I said, "Bend down and touch your toes."

He bent down and touched his toes with absolutely no problem!

I think I was just as amazed as he was. I had never experienced or seen anything like it before. Since that time I have seen hundreds of people healed.

Woman with Blockage in Her Sinus Healed

One day, I was walking down Market Street in Harrisburg, when I saw two young ladies about to pass me. I felt like the Lord wanted me to talk to them. So I stopped them and asked, "Is there anything you need prayer for?"

The ladies were sisters. One was 22-years-old and the other 25. The younger one said that she was born with a complete blockage in her nasal passage. Because of this she has never been able to smell or breathe out her nose. Imagine being born without the use of one of your five senses. Also, when she talked, she sounded very stuffy. Something similar sounding would be if you plugged your own nose and tried to talk.

I asked, "Can I lay my hands over your sinuses—where the blockage is?"

She said, "Yes."

So, I placed my hands over her sinus area and simply said, "In the name of Jesus, blockage be removed."

I stepped back and said, "Test it out."

She tried, and tried but she still couldn't breathe through her nose.

So, I prayed again, "In the name of Jesus, blockage be removed." (When you do this, you don't have to yell or scream. Just speak with the authority God has given you.)

I asked her to try to breathe out of her nose again. This time she was able to take a deep breath from her nose and as she did, you could hear the sound of something in her sinuses breaking up! As she took repeated deep breaths from her nose for the first time in her life, she and her sister looked at each other and started sobbing. They stood there hugging and crying for several minutes. When they were done, I asked, "How do you feel?"

She said, "I can breathe through my nose with my mouth closed for the first time in my life! I can smell for the first time in my life!

I always like to take every opportunity I can to share the good news of Jesus. I figured this was a good opportunity. It turns out, that these two young ladies were already Christians and were attending a church. They both new Jesus as their Savior, but now they know Him as their healer too. That day, they got to experience another side of God they had never experienced before.

This may sound a little strange, but I used to get disappointed when I would strike up a conversation with a stranger—only to find that they were already a Christian. I just wanted to see people saved. I still do, but God taught me early in my walk with Him that there are many Christians He puts in our path who are in need of encouragement and physical healing. I still enjoy seeing people give their hearts to Jesus. Now, I also get a great amount of joy seeing people healed, and seeing my fellow brothers and sisters in Christ encouraged.

Women with Broken Arm and Boy with Deaf Ear Healed

For seven years, I worked as the program director for a Christian after-school program in inner city Harrisburg, called Center for Champions. We would bus kids, grades K-12, in from all over the city and do all sorts of activities with them for a few hours after school each day. Our two main focuses were spiritual and academic. Each day we would help them with their homework, have daily devotions, and weekly chapel services.

When the kids first got to the Center, they would all gather in the large cafeteria-style room. We had about

50 kids, 10-15 volunteers and 6-8 staff members in the room. The first thirty minutes of every day were spent going over announcements, eating snacks, and reciting our weekly memory verse. That week, our memory verse was from Mark 16:17-18 (ICB). The children's version of the Bible I was reading from said:

"Those that believe in Jesus will do these things as proof:…they will lay hands on the sick and the sick will be healed."

I picked this verse for them to memorize because I was planning to teach the kids how to lay hands on the sick and see them healed.

After reciting this verse several times, I saw one of our volunteers sitting at a table. This volunteer had a cast and sling on her right arm. It was a perfect opportunity to put our memory verse into action!

I stopped and in front of everyone asked the volunteer, "What happened to your arm?"

She said, "I slipped on the ice, fell and broke my arm."

I asked, "Can some of the kids and I pray for you?"

She nodded in agreement.

About eight kids gathered around her, laid hands on her arm, and repeated a command after me. "In the name of Jesus, arm be healed."

After that I asked her how her arm felt.

She said, "Some of the pain went away, but it's still really painful."

I remember walking away really disappointed thinking, "God, this was your chance to make the memory verse real to these kids." I dismissed the kids to go to their classes and remained disappointed the rest of the evening.

A few days passed. I had mostly forgotten about praying for the girl's broken arm, but it was still in the back of my mind. That Thursday, during chapel, I taught the kids how to lay hands on the sick and see them healed. At the end, I had all the kids that needed any sort of healing come up on stage. The rest of the kids became the ministry team. That day twelve children came for healing and eleven of them were completely healed! The healings ranged from upset stomachaches, to deaf ears, and everything in-between.

One that really stood out was a boy with a deaf ear. I knew he had trouble hearing, because you often had to repeat what you said to him several times. What I did not know was that he was born 100% deaf in his left ear. I always like to confirm healings whenever possible, so the next day I called his mother.

I asked her how her son was doing and she said, "I don't know what you did, but ever since he came back from Center last night he's been able to hear just fine out of both ears!"

Every few months over the next couple of years I would ask the boy how his ear was. Every time I asked he would say, "I can still hear out of it Mr. Richie."

The following Monday I was so excited about all the healings that took place in chapel that I decided to do the same memory verse again. The kids repeated the Scripture from Mark 16:17-18 (ICB):

"Those that believe in Jesus will do these things as proof:...they will lay hands on the sick and the sick will be healed."

I looked over and saw the same girl who we prayed over the previous week. This time I noticed that she no longer had a cast or sling on her arm.

The thought came to me, "Was she healed when we prayed over her last week, or was it just time for her to get her cast and sling off?"

Then I thought, "There's only one way to find out."

So, in front of everyone, I asked her, "What happened?"

She said, "When you guys prayed for me last week, I had just broke my arm two days before and was still in a lot of pain. When you prayed, some of the pain left, as still in quite a bit of pain. By the time I got ...... from Center, a few hours later, I noticed that all my pain had left. I hadn't taken any pain medicine or anything so I thought it was strange. The next morning, I woke up and there was still no pain in my arm. I called the doctor, and he said that the x-rays clearly showed a break and that I would need the cast on for 6-8 weeks. I asked the doctor if he could take another x-ray. After pressing him a bit he reluctantly agreed, but said, broken arms don't heal in three days. That day, only three days after breaking my arm, I went in for a second x-ray. The doctor came in, holding my original x-ray in one hand and the one taken three days after in the other. He looked at one, then looked at the other. For several minutes he stared back and forth at both x-rays. The longer he looked at them, the more confused he looked. Finally, he looked up at me and said, 'I'm not sure how to explain this, but you don't have a broken arm anymore.' Right then and there, he took off my cast and sling!"

A broken arm was healed after three days with the before and after x-rays to prove it! The doctors said it was impossible, but it happened anyway! This was quite the experience for the 50 or so kids who witnessed this. There were a handful of teens that thought she was an actor and that we paid her to stage the whole thing—I guess you'll always have skeptics, no matter how much proof is given.

This experience taught the kids and I a valuable lesson. Just because someone isn't healed instantly doesn't mean they wont be healed. I would say the majority of time I minister to someone they are healed instantly, but over the years I have had many people who experience the fullness of their healing a few hours later, some the next day, and others a few days later. For this reason, I never pull back my faith when someone isn't instantly healed—I keep believing until the healing manifests.

Demon Cast Out
A Deaf, Mute Man Healed

A few years ago, I volunteered at a food ministry in the city. This ministry would hand out grocery bags of food to the needy. My job was to stand in front of the line and offer prayer to people as they waited. There was about 150 people that came and about 100 of them said "yes" to prayer. We had 90 minutes to hand out all the grocery bags, so that left me with about 1 minute to pray with each person! (I had an absolute blast doing this, by the way.)

One day, while volunteering, a man came up to me. I asked him the same question I had asked everyone else that day. "Is there anything you need prayer for today, sir?"

The man looked at me, pointed to his ears and said something in gibberish.

MOVING MOUNTAINS

At first, I thought the man was speaking another language—but it didn't sound like any language I had ever heard before.

I asked him again, "Sir, do you have a prayer request?"

This time the man looked at me, and you could tell he was annoyed. He mumbled something in gibberish and pointed at his ears even more emphatically.

All of a sudden, it struck me. This man is deaf and mute! So I laid my hands on his head and said, "In the name of Jesus, ears be opened and tongue be loosed." I then whispered in his ear, "Jesus loves you," to see if he could hear me.

The man continued to speak in gibberish and point to his ears.

I repeated, "In the name of Jesus, ears be opened and tongue be loosed." a few more times—each time with the same result.

I was about ready to give up when I heard the Holy Spirit speak to me saying, "Cast out a deaf and mute spirit."

So I put my hand on the man's head again and simply said, "Deaf and mute spirit come out." (An important side note: The same principals that apply to healing the sick also apply to casting out demons). I said this three times. It did not take hours of deliverance like you see in the movies. It literally took a few second didn't yell or scream. I just spoke in my normal tone of voice. After the third time saying this, the man began to laugh hysterically! He was laughing as if I had just told him the funniest joke he had ever heard! I was a bit taken back by his reaction. I had seen many people cry when they are healed, I have seen many people jump up and down for joy or scream, and shout when they were healed, but I had never seen anyone laugh—especially like this! (Several weeks later I was reading one of Randy Clark's manuals on healing and deliverance and found out that laughter can be a sign of the Holy Spirit at work in the body of a demonically oppressed person.)[1]

After laughing the man straightened up, looked at me with a serious face and said "I can hear now! I can speak now! I can hear now! I can speak now!" The man kept repeating this over and over again. We tested it out by whispering several different things in his ears and each time he repeated them perfectly. The next thing I knew the man was off to get his groceries.

I was so excited that when I got home I called everyone I could to tell them what happened. However, as the days went by I remember thinking to myself, "Did that really just happen?" I new it did, but when you see something that you've only read about in the Bible, it's a very surreal experience!

A few weeks later I went back hoping to see the same guy again. Sure enough, he was there! As he approached me, I struggled to figure out what to say to him. So, I said the first thing that came to my mind, "Do you remember me?" I asked.

The man looked at me and said, "How could I ever forget you? You're the one who prayed for me. Now I can hear and now I can speak!"

—END NOTE—

1. Randy Clark, *Global Awakening Ministry Team Training Manual*, (Global Awakening, 2009), page 95.

chapter three

Speaking to Your Mountain

Soon after my experience with God on Saturday, September 18, 2010 I decided to search for confirmation in the Bible. God had spoken to me clearly and what He told me was working extremely well, but I still wanted to make sure that it lined up with Scripture.

I decided to read through the four gospels and the book of Acts and study how Jesus and the Apostles healed the sick. I had read through these books many times, but never with that particular focus.

What I found confirmed everything that God had told me about *declaring* healing over the sick, instead of *praying* and asking God to heal the sick.

Throughout the gospels and the book of Acts there are literally dozens of examples of how Jesus and the Apostles healed the sick. What I found, was not once did they actually pray and ask God to heal!

Instead, I found dozens of examples where Jesus and the Apostles *declared* healing over people, saying things like, "Be opened," to blind eyes and deaf ears or, "Jesus heals you, get up and walk," to bedridden and paralyzed individuals.

Lets look at four examples from Scripture that illustrate what I am saying. (I would encourage you to read through the four gospels, and the book of Acts yourself, with the focus on how Jesus and the Apostles healed the sick).

> *"Again, departing from the region of Tyre and Sidon, He (Jesus) came through the midst of the region of Decapolis to the Sea of Galilee. Then they brought to Him one who was deaf and had an impediment in his speech, and they begged Him to put His hand on him. And He took him aside from the multitude, and put His fingers in his ears, and He spat and touched his tongue. Then, looking up to heaven, He sighed, and said to him, "Ephphatha," that is, "Be opened." Immediately his ears were opened, and the impediment of his tongue was loosed, and he spoke plainly"* (Mark 7:31-35).

In this passage a deaf, mute man was brought to Jesus. Did Jesus pray, begging God, "Father, please heal this deaf mute man."? No! Jesus spoke to the situation, saying, "Be opened," and the man was able to hear and speak. You never see Jesus begging or asking God to heal. Instead, what you see is Jesus speaking to the situation and commanding healing to take place. Let's look at another example from Jesus' ministry.

> *"Now He (Jesus) arose from the synagogue and entered Simon's house. But Simon's wife's mother was sick with a high fever, and they made request of Him concerning her. So He stood over her and rebuked the fever, and it left her. And immediately she arose and served them"* (Luke 4:38-39).

Again, did Jesus pray, begging God, "Father, please heal this women and take away her fever."? No! Jesus rebuked the fever and the fever left. As a side note, the word rebuke does not mean that Jesus literally said, "I rebuke you fever." The word rebuke in this context means that Jesus spoke to the fever and told it what to do. In other words, Jesus commanded the fever to leave and it left.

Let's look at two examples from Scripture where the Apostles healed the sick in the book of Acts.

> *"Now Peter and John went up together to the temple at the hour of prayer, the ninth hour. And*

a certain man lame from his mother's womb was carried, whom they laid daily at the gate of the temple which is called Beautiful, to ask alms from those who entered the temple; who, seeing Peter and John about to go into the temple, asked for alms. And fixing his eyes on him, with John, Peter said, "Look at us." So he gave them his attention, expecting to receive something from them. Then Peter said, "Silver and gold I do not have, <u>but what I do have I give you: In the name of Jesus Christ of Nazareth, rise up and walk.</u>" And he took him by the right hand and lifted him up, and immediately his feet and ankle bones received strength. So he, leaping up, stood and walked and entered the temple with them—walking, leaping, and praising God" (Acts 3:1-8).

On their way to the temple, Peter and John saw a man who was lame since birth. This man was crippled and unable to walk. He was outside the temple begging for money. When Peter and John ministered healing to this man, did they pray something like, "Father, if it be thy will, please heal this man."? No! They said, "In the name of Jesus Christ, get up and walk!" Then they grabbed the man by the hands and helped him to his feet. As they did this, the man regained strength in his legs and was healed! They did not beg God for healing, nor did they question God's will to heal this man. They didn't even ask God to heal this man. They simply spoke to the situation and commanded the man to be healed.

Let's look at one more example from the book of Acts.

"Now it came to pass, as Peter went through all parts of the country, that he also came down to the saints who dwelt in Lydda. There he found a certain man named Aeneas, who had been bedridden eight years and was paralyzed. And Peter said to him, "Aeneas, Jesus the Christ heals you. Arise and make your bed." Then he arose immediately. So all who dwelt at Lydda and Sharon saw him and turned to the Lord" (Acts 9:32-35).

In this passage, Peter came across a man who had been paralyzed and bedridden for eight years. How did Peter minister healing to this man? Did he pray, "Father please heal this man."? No! Peter simply looked at the man and said, "Jesus Christ heals you. Arise and make your bed." Then, the man got up and began to walk!

There is something else we can learn from this passage. Acts 9:35 says that as a result of this one man's healing, all who lived in this town gave their lives to Jesus! For many people, physical healing is a powerful sign that Jesus is real and that the gospel is true.

I've seen many times where I've asked someone if I could pray for them and they've said, "No thanks, I'm an atheist," or "No thanks, I don't believe in miracles." Many times I will encourage them by saying something like: "What have you got to lose? If I pray for you and nothing happens, then all you've done is waste a couple of minutes. But, if I pray for you and you're healed, then you'll be free from the sickness."

I've had many encounters with people like this that end up allowing me to pray for them and then I get to see them healed! I've seen many unbelievers, even atheists, come to Christ this way.

Let's look at another Scripture. In this passage, found in the gospel of Matthew, we find the disciples attempting to heal the sick. They had been with Jesus for a little while and had seen Him heal countless people. Now, it was their turn to minister healing, but they failed. At the end of this passage Jesus teaches them a very valuable lesson concerning how to heal the sick. Let's read Matthew 17:14-20:

> "And when they had come to the multitude, a man came to Him (Jesus), kneeling down to Him and saying, "Lord, have mercy on my son, for he is an epileptic and suffers severely; for he often falls into the fire and often into the water. So I brought him to Your disciples, but they could not cure him."
>
> Then Jesus answered and said, "O faithless and perverse generation, how long shall I be with you? How long shall I bear with you? Bring him here to Me." And Jesus rebuked the demon, and

> *it came out of him; and the child was cured from that very hour.*
>
> *Then the disciples came to Jesus privately and said, "Why could we not cast it out?"*
>
> *So Jesus said to them, "Because of your unbelief, for assuredly, I say to you, if you have faith as a mustard seed, you will **say** to this mountain, 'Move from here to there,' and it will move; and nothing will be impossible for you."*

In Matthew 17:20, Jesus said that if we *speak* to our mountain it will move from here to there. First, what is the mountain Jesus is referring to? In the context of this Scripture, the mountain is demon possession and epilepsy. But in a broader sense, a mountain can be demon possession, any sickness, disease or injury. And it can also mean any obstacle that is in your pathway.

How did Jesus say we would heal the sick and cast out demons? Did He say, "If you pray and ask God to move the mountain, God will move it."? No! He said if we *speak* to the mountain, the mountain will be moved!

I have the privilege of going to different churches and teaching this. I also teach this at a local ministry school. Several years ago, a student at the ministry school asked me a question after class. He said, "So what about James 5:14? It clearly tells us to *pray* for the sick. It never says anything about speaking to sickness."

I've always been taught, if you don't have an answer to someone's question don't try to make one up. Simply tell them, "I don't know." So, that's what I did. I told him that it was a very good question and I would try to find an answer for him.

One night, while reading the Bible, God gave me the answer to this question. I started reading some Psalms, was then led to Proverbs, and somehow ended up in James chapter 5.

That's when I felt the Holy Spirit tell me, "I'm going to give you the answer to the student's question." Holy Spirit proceeded to speak to me saying, "A lot of times when people quote Scripture they quote only a single verse or two and take it out of context (I think we are all guilty of doing this from time to time, unintentionally.) Read the entire chapter of James 5 in context, and I will give you the answer to his question."

So I read James chapter 5 in context. The verses that the Holy Spirit spoke to me about were verses 13-18, which read:

> *"Is anyone among you suffering? Let him **pray**. Is anyone cheerful? Let him sing psalms. Is anyone among you sick? Let him call for the elders of the church, and let them **pray** over him, anointing him with oil in the name of the Lord. And the **prayer** of faith will save the sick, and the Lord will raise him up. And if he has committed*

*sins, he will be forgiven. Confess your trespasses to one another, and **pray** for one another, that you may be healed. The effective, fervent **prayer** of a righteous man avails much. Elijah was a man with a nature like ours, and he **prayed** earnestly that it would not rain; and it did not rain on the land for three years and six months. And he **prayed** again, and the heaven gave rain, and the earth produced its fruit."*

There are few things I want to point out. First of all, it does say to pray. In these six verses, the word *pray*, *prayer* or *prayed* is mentioned seven times. It never mentions commanding or speaking to sickness. Not even once. So what's the deal? Does the Bible contradict itself by telling us to "*speak* to sickness and disease" in one passage, and "*pray* for the sick" in another? Let's find out.

The key verses the Holy Spirit highlighted to me were verses 17 and 18. In this passage, James compares the elders' prayer of faith for healing with Elijah's prayer that it would not rain for three and a half years *and* with Elijah praying after a three and a half year period of time that it would rain again.

The Holy Spirit spoke to me again saying, "How did Elijah pray?" I responded, "I remember the story but I can't remember how he prayed." The Holy Spirit said, "Read the story again." So I turned my Bible to 1 Kings 17:1-7 which says:

> *"And Elijah the Tishbite, of the inhabitants of Gilead, said to Ahab, "As the Lord God of Israel lives, before whom I stand, there shall not be dew nor rain these years, except at my word."*
>
> *Then the word of the Lord came to him, saying, "Get away from here and turn eastward, and hide by the Brook Cherith, which flows into the Jordan. And it will be that you shall drink from the brook, and I have commanded the ravens to feed you there."*
>
> *So he went and did according to the word of the Lord, for he went and stayed by the Brook Cherith, which flows into the Jordan. The ravens brought him bread and meat in the morning, and bread and meat in the evening; and he drank from the brook. And it happened after a while that the brook dried up, because there had been no rain in the land."*

Did you see it? How did Elijah pray? Did he pray asking God, "Lord please let it not rain for three and a half years."? No! Elijah's prayer is found in verse 1. Let's read it again. Elijah said:

> *"...As the Lord God of Israel lives, before whom I stand,* **there shall not be dew nor rain these years, except at my word"** (Kings 17:1).

Elijah's prayer was not a prayer of asking or begging God to do something. Elijah's prayer was a command.

It was a declaration that it would not rain for three and a half years. Guess what happened? It did not rain for three and a half years! Elijah did not pray and ask God to stop the rain. He commanded the weather and the weather listened to him.

This reminds me of the story of Jesus and the disciples crossing the Sea of Galilee in Luke 8:22-25:

"Now it happened, on a certain day, that He (Jesus) got into a boat with His disciples. And He said to them, "Let us cross over to the other side of the lake." And they launched out. But as they sailed He fell asleep. And a windstorm came down on the lake, and they were filling with water, and were in jeopardy. And they came to Him and awoke Him, saying, "Master, Master, we are perishing!"

Then He arose and rebuked the wind and the raging of the water. And they ceased, and there was a calm. But He said to them, "Where is your faith?"

And they were afraid, and marveled, saying to one another, "Who can this be? For He commands even the winds and water, and they obey Him!"

Two points I want to highlight from this Scripture. First, notice that Jesus *rebuked* the wind and the waves. He did not pray and ask His Father to calm the storm. Jesus *spoke* to the storm and the storm was calmed.

Secondly, after Jesus calmed the storm, He turned to His disciples and said, *"Where is your faith?"* What was Jesus implying when He asked His disciples this question? Jesus was basically saying, *"Why did you wake me up? You could have done the same thing!"*

This principle of speaking to your mountain, as opposed to begging and asking God to remove it for you, applies to many other areas — not just healing the sick, casting out demons and commanding wind, rain or storms to cease.

Here's one example:

A couple of years ago, I was teaching this topic for an entire month at a local church. At the end of class, I had everyone get into small groups and pray for each other. They could pray for each other concerning anything. It could be for physical healing or any other need. I also had them pray using this principal of speaking to the problem instead of asking, or begging God to take the problem away. After they prayed, I asked them what they prayed for. About 5 or 6 people where praying for jobs. The following Wednesday, I started class by asking for testimonies concerning answers to prayer. Guess what? Every single person that prayed for a job had gotten one over the past week! One young lady was so excited because a few hours before our last class, she had an interview at a place that she really wanted to work. By the time she got home after class, she had a message on her answering machine saying that she got the job!

Again, I want to emphasize the importance of speaking to your mountain instead of begging God to remove it. There is power in the words you speak! Proverbs 18:21 says:

> *"Death and life are in the power of the tongue, And those who love it will eat its fruit."*

Now lets take a look at 1 Kings 18:41-46. Three and a half years had passed since Elijah's declaration that it would not rain (1 Kings 17:1-7). There had been a long drought. Now it was time for it to rain.

> *"Then Elijah said to Ahab, "Go up, eat and drink; for there is the sound of abundance of rain." So Ahab went up to eat and drink. And Elijah went up to the top of Carmel; then he bowed down on the ground, and put his face between his knees, and said to his servant, "Go up now, look toward the sea."*
>
> *So he went up and looked, and said, "There is nothing." And seven times he said, "Go again."*
>
> *Then it came to pass the seventh time, that he said, "There is a cloud, as small as a man's hand, rising out of the sea!" So he said, "Go up, say to Ahab, 'Prepare your chariot, and go down before the rain stops you.'"*

Now it happened in the meantime that the sky became black with clouds and wind, and there was a heavy rain. So Ahab rode away and went to Jezreel. Then the hand of the Lord came upon Elijah; and he girded up his loins and ran ahead of Ahab to the entrance of Jezreel."

How did Elijah pray? His prayer is found in verse 41:

"Go up, eat and drink; **for there is the sound of abundance of rain."**

Again, Elijah did not beg God to send the rain. Instead, he spoke, saying that he heard the sound of abundant rain, even though it was not raining and had not rained for three and a half years!

Verse 43 says that when they looked out, it still was not raining. So, Elijah said again, "I hear the sound of abundant rain!" He said this seven times. Each time they went up and looked, there was no rain. But on the seventh time Elijah spoke, a small cloud formed. The winds began to pick up and it started to rain!

Elijah's prayer was not a prayer of asking God to let the rain fall, but a declaration that, *"There is the sound of abundant rain."*

Elijah was calling forth things that where not, as though they were. *That is what the Bible calls the prayer of faith* as we read in Romans 4:17. This is also how the elders prayed for the sick in James chapter 5.

chapter four

The Authority that *EVERY* Believer Has

I remember, as a young Christian in Bible school, striving to receive the gift of healing. For many years, I thought that the gift of healing was something I had to obtain. I thought I had to fast enough, pray enough, and be a good enough person to obtain it. I thought I had to earn the ability to lay hands on the sick and see them healed.

I really didn't start seeing people healed until I came to understand that its not about obtaining this ability, but rather knowing that everything I need is *already* within me. I already had the ability to heal the sick I just never knew it!

The gifts of the Spirit are all freely given. They can't be earned any more than salvation can (Ephesians 2:8-9).

Otherwise we would be able to brag every time we saw someone healed (or operated in any of the gifts). We could say that we earned this ability by fasting enough, praying enough or being a good enough person. But, as you will see in this chapter, healing the sick is something every believer can do. No one can brag about it. The reason we can all heal the sick is because of the authority we have *all* been given.

I have a lot of Scriptures that I want to share, to support my point. Let's look at Luke 9:1-2. In this passage we see Jesus giving His twelve disciples power and authority to cast out demons and heal the sick.

> *"Then He called His twelve disciples together and gave them **power** and **authority** over all demons, and to cure diseases. He sent them to preach the kingdom of God and to heal the sick."*

Some people believe that the power and authority to cast out demons and heal the sick was just given to the original twelve disciples. This however, is not true. One chapter later, in Luke 10:17-19, we see Jesus giving this same power and authority to a much broader group of people. Let's read:

> *"Then the **seventy** returned with joy, saying, "Lord, even the demons are subject to us in Your name."*
>
> *And He said to them, "I saw Satan fall like lightning from heaven. Behold, I give you the*

***authority** to trample on serpents and scorpions, and over all the power of the enemy, and nothing shall by any means hurt you."*

Here we see a group of *SEVENTY* followers of Jesus rejoicing because they have been given this authority! Lets keep going. Lets look at Mark 9:38-40:

"Now John answered Him, saying, "Teacher, we saw someone who does not follow us casting out demons in Your name, and we forbade him because he does not follow us."

But Jesus said, "Do not forbid him, for no one who works a miracle in My name can soon afterward speak evil of Me. For he who is not against us is on our side."

This passage is a bit comical to me. Here we see some random man going around casting out demons and performing miracles in Jesus name! This man was not part of the twelve or the seventy. He's just an anonymous person who believes in Jesus, and walks in the same power and authority as the twelve disciples.

John, not knowing who this man was, came up to him and forbade him to do these things because he was not a part of their group. How did Jesus respond? Jesus said, *"Do not forbid him, for no one who works a miracle in My name can soon afterward speak evil of Me. For he who is not against us is on our side."* He said that this man was on there side!

MOVING MOUNTAINS

Now let's take a look at one of my favorite Scriptures. This Scripture includes an even broader group than the twelve and the seventy. Mark 16:15-18 says:

*"And He said to them, "Go into all the world and preach the gospel to every creature. He who believes and is baptized will be saved; but he who does not believe will be condemned. And these signs will follow those who **believe**: In My name they will cast out demons; they will speak with new tongues; they will take up serpents; and if they drink anything deadly, it will by no means hurt them; they will lay hands on the sick, and they will recover."*

Did you see that? The key part of this Scripture is the first part of verse 17, which says, *"And these signs will follow those who **believe**."*

It doesn't say, "And these signs will follow the pastors."

It doesn't say, "And these signs will follow the evangelists."

It doesn't say, "And these signs will follow the apostles."

It doesn't say, "And these signs will follow those in full time ministry."

It doesn't say, "And these signs will follow the select few special people that I choose and give the gift to."

It says *"And these signs will follow those who believe."* The ONLY requirement mentioned to cast out demons and heal the sick is that you believe! *I am a believer!*

Let me ask you a few questions? Are you a follower of Jesus Christ? Do you believe that you can cast out demons and heal the sick? If you answered, "Yes" to both of those questions, then you are qualified to cast out demons and heal the sick.

Those are the ONLY two questions you need to answer to find out if you are qualified to do this stuff! The biggest reason most Christians fail to walk in this power and authority is because they don't believe they have this power and authority. They believe that casting out demons and healing the sick is not for today. They believe that it's something that only the original twelve Apostles were able to do. Some even believe that this power and authority are for today, but only for a select group of "Christian superstars" whom God handpicks.

This mindset has to change! This world is waiting for the body of Christ to rise up and become ALL that God has created her to be! There is a world full of people who are hurting and dying every day—people who are ripe and ready to receive the good news! Too many of us think that it's someone else's job to share the gospel, heal the sick and set the captives free.

Can you tell I'm passionate about this? It's because over the past fifteen years I've seen it with my own eyes. I'm addicted to evangelism. I see the hurting and the dying every day! And I see how ripe and ready they are to receive the good news about Jesus. But too many of us are too afraid to share the gospel and lay hands on the sick. Fear has crippled the Church. Because of this, each day, thousands of people go off into eternity without a relationship with Jesus Christ.

Please listen! God has no plan B! We, (the body of Christ), are it! We are plan A. There is no other plan. For the sake of the world, we need to overcome our fear and step out! When we start doing that, we will become ALL that God has created us to be!

Let's move on and read another one of my favorite Scriptures John 14:12, which says:

> "Most assuredly, I say to you, he who **believes** in Me (Jesus), the works that I do he will do also; and greater works than these he will do, because I go to My Father."

Wow! What a statement by Jesus! I remember reading this verse as a newly saved Christian and thinking, "This can't mean what it says. There has to be some hidden meaning behind it." Then I remember God speaking to me loud and clear, saying, "No! I mean what I say and I say what I mean!"

Sometimes we have to take what God says at face value. And John 14:12 clearly says that if you are a believer in Jesus Christ, you can do the *SAME* things Jesus did. Even greater things!

I am starting to see some of the *same* things. But still, have a hard time wrapping my mind around the *greater* things. I've heard many people give examples of what they think are the greater works. But, as far as I know, they are all speculation. Its one of those mysteries I hope to find out someday in this lifetime!

Let's look at some of the "same works." What do you think Jesus is talking about when He says believers will do the same things He did? For me, it's not too hard to figure out. As you read the four Gospels, you will notice that they are dominated by accounts of Jesus healing the sick, casting out demons, performing miracles, and preaching the gospel.

Again we see in John 14:12, just like we saw in Mark 16:15-18, that the only qualification required to do these same works (i.e., healing the sick, casting out demons, performing miracles and preaching the gospel) is to believe in Jesus! If you believe in Jesus, then you are qualified! It's really as simple as that!

Again, I want to emphasis that this ability was not just for the original twelve disciples. It was not just for the seventy. It's not just for the random select few! Jesus gave power and authority over the devil, demons, sickness & disease to *EVERY BELIEVER!* Me.

There's a powerful Scripture that really drives this point home. It's found in Mark 13:32-37, as follows:

> *"But of that day and hour no one knows, not even the angels in heaven, nor the Son, but only the Father. Take heed, watch and pray; for you do not know when the time is. It is like a man going to a far country, who left his house and **gave authority to his servants**, and to each his work, and commanded the doorkeeper to watch. Watch therefore, for you do not know when the master of the house is coming—in the evening, at midnight, at the crowing of the rooster, or in the morning—lest, coming suddenly, he find you sleeping. And what I say to you, I say to all: Watch!"*

In this Scripture, Jesus is talking to His disciples about the time between His ascension to heaven, which took place 2,000 years ago (Acts 1:6-11) and the time of His return, which has not happened yet. In other words, Jesus is talking about the times we are living in today.

In verse 34, Jesus likens Himself to a man that has gone to a far off country (heaven). While He is gone, He has given His servants (you and I) *His* authority. In other words, Jesus is saying that between the time of His ascension and the time of His return, He has given us (the body of Christ) *His* authority!

To gain a clearer understanding of what Jesus is telling us, let's look at the Greek word used for authority in this passage. The word used for authority is "Exousia" (Pronounced "Ex-oo-see-ah") which means:

A) Power—As in, Jesus gave us *His* power.

B) Ability—As in, Jesus gave us *His* ability.

C) Authority—As in, Jesus gave us *His* authority.[1]

How can we expect to do the same works as Jesus, and even greater works (John 14:12)? We have the *same* power, ability and authority over the devil, demons, sickness and disease that Jesus has! Verse 35-37 says that when He comes back, He expects to find us using all three!

Psalm 8 puts it this way:

"O Lord, our Lord, your majestic name fills the earth! Your glory is higher than the heavens. You have taught children and infants to tell of your strength, silencing your enemies and all who oppose you.

When I look at the night sky and see the work of your fingers—the moon and the stars you set in place—what are mere mortals that you should think about them, human beings that you should care for them? ***Yet you made them only a little lower than God and crowned them with glory*** *and honor. You gave them charge of everything you made, putting all things under their authority—the flocks and the herds and all the wild animals, the birds in the sky, the fish in the sea, and everything that swims the ocean currents.*

O Lord, our Lord, your majestic name fills the earth!" (NLT)

Verse 5 says that we were made just a little bit lower than God. And verse 6 says that God put us in charge over everything He created. The Psalm goes on to list some of the things we have been given authority over.

Hebrews 2:8 (quoting Psalm 8) says:

"You gave them (man) *authority over **all things.*** *Now when it says "all things," it means **nothing** is left out...."* (NLT)

In other words, if God created it, we have authority over it! And as you know, God is the creator of *ALL* things.

One of my favorite Bible teachers, Curry Blake, once listed the ranking of authority in the universe this way:

A) God

B) Redeemed man (Christians)

C) Angels

D) Demons (including the devil)

E) Unredeemed man (The unsaved)[2]

This fits perfectly with Psalm 8 and Hebrews 2:8 and also Ephesians 1:19-23 which reads:

"and what is the exceeding greatness of His power toward us who believe, according to the working of His mighty power which He worked in Christ when He raised Him from the dead and seated Him at His right hand in the heavenly places, far above all principality and power and might and dominion, and every name that is named, not only in this age but also in that which is to come.

And He put all things under His feet, and gave Him to be head over all things to the church, which is His body, the fullness of Him who fills all in all."

Ephesians Chapter 2:1-6

"And you He made alive, who were dead in trespasses and sins, in which you once walked according to the course of this world, according to the prince of the power of the air, the spirit who now works in the sons of disobedience, among whom also we all once conducted ourselves in the lusts of our flesh, fulfilling the desires of the

flesh and of the mind, and were by nature children of wrath, just as the others.

But God, who is rich in mercy, <u>because of His great love with which He loved us</u>, even when we were dead in trespasses, <u>m<u>ade us alive together with Christ</u></u> (by grace you have been saved), **and raised us up together, and made us sit together in the heavenly places in Christ Jesus."**

According to this passage, where is Jesus right now? It says that He is seated in <u>heaven</u> at *<u>God's right hand</u>*, far above all principalities and powers and *EVERYTHING* that has a name!

The "right hand of God" represents God's ultimate power and authority.³

According to this passage, where are you right now? Yes, you are here on earth. But did you also know that you are seated in heaven *WITH Jesus at Gods right hand* (The place of God's ultimate power and authority)(Ephesians 2:6)? You (as a believer) are seated in the *same place* of power and authority as Jesus! And as Ephesians says, we (like Jesus) are also seated far above *ALL* principalities, powers and *EVERYTHING* that has a name!

Does the devil have a name? Yes!

Do the demons have a name? Yes!

Does cancer have a name? Yes!

Does diabetes have a name? Yes!

If it has a name, you have authority over it! We were created to have dominion over everything God created and, God created everything. This was God's original plan in the Garden of Eden (Genesis 1:26-28). In the Garden, man was deceived into giving up his authority. At the cross, Jesus ripped it from the enemy's hands and gave it back to us!

END NOTES

1. *The New Strong's Exhaustive Concordance of the Bible (Strongs #1849)*, (Nashville, TN: Thomas Nelson Publishers, 1990), page 90.

2. http://www.divinerevelations.info/documents/healing/jgl/jgl_ministries.htm. Accessed April 28, 2016.

3. https://www.biblegateway.com/resources/dictionary-of-bible-themes/1270-right-hand-God. Accessed April 28, 2016.

chapter five

Healing and Atonement

Before we dig into the Scriptures, I want to define the word "Atonement." According to the *New Bible Dictionary*, the word "atonement" means:

> "A making at one. It points to a process of bringing those who are estranged into unity. It's used to denote the work of Christ in dealing with the problem posed by the sin of man and bringing sinners into right relation with God."[1]

The *New Bible Dictionary* continues,

> "The need for atonement is brought about by three things: the universality of sin, the seriousness of sin, and man's inability to deal with sin."[2]

When we talk about the atonement in the context of the New Testament, we are talking about how Jesus dealt with sin, including all the issues that came with sin and reconciled man back to God.

Some would argue that the atonement had nothing to do with physical healing—it had only to do with the forgiveness of sins. Yet, Scripture makes it clear that physical healing is indeed a part of what Jesus did for us on the cross.

When talking about this subject, we need to look back in Genesis at the fall of man. Let's start with Genesis 2:8-17:

"The Lord God planted a garden eastward in Eden, and there He put the man whom He had formed. And out of the ground the Lord God made every tree grow that is pleasant to the sight and good for food. The tree of life was also in the midst of the garden, and the tree of the knowledge of good and evil.

Now a river went out of Eden to water the garden, and from there it parted and became four riverheads. The name of the first is Pishon; it is the one which skirts the whole land of Havilah, where there is gold. And the gold of that land is good. Bdellium and the onyx stone are there. The name of the second river is Gihon; it is the one which goes around the whole land of Cush. The name of the third river is Hiddekel; it is the one which goes toward the east of Assyria. The fourth river is the Euphrates.

Then the Lord God took the man and put him in the garden of Eden to tend and keep it. And the Lord God commanded the man, saying, "Of every tree of the garden you may freely eat; but of the tree of the knowledge of good and evil you shall not eat, for in the day that you eat of it you shall surely die."

God had one rule in the Garden of Eden. That one rule was to not eat from the tree of the knowledge of good and evil. If they were to break that rule, it would ultimately bring them death.

Now, let's take a look at Genesis 3:1-8:

"Now the serpent was more cunning than any beast of the field which the Lord God had made. And he said to the woman, "Has God indeed said, 'You shall not eat of every tree of the garden'?"

And the woman said to the serpent, "We may eat the fruit of the trees of the garden; but of the fruit of the tree which is in the midst of the garden, God has said, 'You shall not eat it, nor shall you touch it, lest you die.' "

Then the serpent said to the woman, "You will not surely die. For God knows that in the day you eat of it your eyes will be opened, and you will be like God, knowing good and evil."

So when the woman saw that the tree was good for food, that it was pleasant to the eyes, and a tree desirable to make one wise, she took of its fruit and ate. She also gave to her husband with her, and he ate. Then the eyes of both of them were opened, and they knew that they were naked; and they sewed fig leaves together and made themselves coverings.

And they heard the sound of the Lord God walking in the garden in the cool of the day, and Adam and his wife hid themselves from the presence of the Lord God among the trees of the garden."

Adam and Eve both sinned by eating the forbidden fruit and that sin led to separation from God, sickness, disease and ultimately death.

Which came first; separation from God, sickness, disease, death or sin? I think we all know the answer to that question, but let's take a look at what the Bible says:

*"Therefore, just as through one man sin entered the world, and **death through sin**, and thus death spread to all men, because all sinned"* (Romans 5:12).

Sin entered the world first, and then because of sin; sickness, disease and death followed. Because of

Adams sin; sin, sickness, disease and death spread to all humanity.

Romans 6:23 says:

"...the wages (or the price we pay) for sin is death..."

Sin, sickness, disease and death are all intertwined. We know that Jesus died on the cross for our sins, but because sin, sickness, disease and death are all connected together, when Jesus died on the cross it wasn't just for our sins. He also died for the consequences of our sins, which was separation from God, sickness, disease and death.

Romans 8:2 says:

*"For the law of the Spirit of life in Christ Jesus has made me free from the law of **sin and death**."*

There is no separating sin and death. They are two sides of the same coin. As Romans 8:2 says, Jesus came to free us from both of them! If Jesus came to free us from both sin and death, you would expect to find Jesus spending the majority of His earthly ministry doing two things:

1. Forgiving people of their sins.

2. Healing people of sickness and disease.

And this is exactly what you find Jesus doing when you read the gospels!

The gospels are filled with stories of Jesus forgiving people of their sins and healing them of sickness and disease. Here's just one:

> *"So He got into a boat, crossed over, and came to His own city. Then behold, they brought to Him a paralytic lying on a bed. When Jesus saw their faith, He said to the paralytic, "Son, be of good cheer; your sins are forgiven you."*
>
> *And at once some of the scribes said within themselves, "This Man blasphemes!"*
>
> *But Jesus, knowing their thoughts, said, "Why do you think evil in your hearts? For which is easier, to say, 'Your sins are forgiven you,' or to say, 'Arise and walk'? But that you may know that the Son of Man has power on earth to forgive sins"—then He said to the paralytic, "Arise, take up your bed, and go to your house." And he arose and departed to his house.*
>
> *Now when the multitudes saw it, they marveled and glorified God, who had given such power to men"* (Matthew 9:1-8).

This is just one example of many. The gospels are packed with dozens of stories of Jesus forgiving people of their sins and healing their sick bodies. As a matter of fact, this is what Jesus did everywhere He went!

1 John 3:8 says that the reason Jesus came to earth was to destroy the works of the devil. Acts 10:38 says Jesus went about doing good, and healing ALL who were oppressed by the devil.

According to Acts 10:38, sickness is oppression by the devil. According to 1 John 3:8, Jesus came to destroy the works of the devil. This is why you see Jesus "going about" healing *EVERYONE* He came in contact with. Healing the sick is an act of warfare against the kingdom of darkness.

John G. Lake, one of the great faith healers of the 20th century, once said:

> "God is as willing to heal as He is to save. Healing is a part of salvation. It is not separate from salvation. Healing was purchased by the blood of Jesus."[3]

Let's take a look at one of the most well known Scripture in the entire Bible. Can you guess what it is? It's a verse that almost every Christian and non-Christians alike can quote from memory with ease. You've got it! It's John 3:16. While we are going to read John 3:16, it's really the verse that follows it that we need to take a closer look at.

> *"For God so loved the world that He gave His only begotten Son, that whoever believes in Him should not perish but have everlasting life. For God did not send His Son into the world to*

condemn the world, but that the world through Him might be saved" (John 3:16-17).

Most of us have been taught that John 3:16 is about how Jesus died on the cross for our sins so that we could go to heaven one day. While this is true, this is only part of the truth. There is a lot more to this Scripture!

Verse 17 says:

*"For God did not send His Son into the world to condemn the world, but that the world through Him might be **saved**."*

The key word is the word "saved." What do you think of when you hear the word "saved"? Do you think of forgiveness of sins? Do you think of being set free from sin? Do you think of having a relationship with God? Do you think of going to heaven one day when you die? If you answered, "Yes," then you are correct. But, is that all you think of? If so, I'm here to tell you that to be saved means so much more than all of the things I just mentioned!

The word "saved," in the language of the New Testament, was originally written in the ancient Greek. The word used for "saved" is the Greek word "sozo."[4] "Sozo" also means to deliver, heal and protect. It means to make well and to make whole. "Sozo" is an all-encompassing word, which includes restoring the body, soul and spirit of a person!

In other words, Jesus did not just die on the cross so that we could go to heaven one day. He died so that we could receive *everything* that was stolen from us in the Garden of Eden!

Romans 5:6-11 says:

"For when we were still without strength, in due time Christ died for the ungodly. For scarcely for a righteous man will one die; yet perhaps for a good man someone would even dare to die. But God demonstrates His own love toward us, in that while we were still sinners, Christ died for us. Much more then, having now been justified by His blood, we shall be saved from wrath through Him. For if when we were enemies we were reconciled to God through the death of His Son, much more, having been reconciled, we shall be saved by His life. And not only that, but we also rejoice in God through our Lord Jesus Christ, through whom we have now received the reconciliation."

In verses 9 and 10, the same Greek word for "saved" (sozo) is used as in John 3:17. Again, "sozo" means to save, deliver, heal and protect. It means to make well and to make whole—body, soul and spirit.

Notice the King James Version verse 11 reads:

*"We also rejoice in God through our Lord Jesus Christ, through whom we have now received the **Atonement**."*

The Greek word used for "atonement" in this passage means to:

Exchange – As in, Jesus exchanged His life for ours.

Reconcile – As in, Jesus reconciled us body, soul and spirit to Himself.

Restore – As in, Jesus restored ALL things back to us that were taken in the Garden of Eden.[5]

Because of what Jesus did for you on the cross:

- You have a right to a relationship with God!

- You have a right to deliverance and freedom!

- You have a right to physical healing!

Healing *IS* salvation to the physical body. It is your blood bought right as a son or daughter of God!

1 Peter 2:24 says:

"who Himself bore our sins in His own body on the tree, that we, having died to sins, might live for righteousness—by whose stripes you were healed."

Here, the apostle Peter quotes a popular verse from the Old Testament Isaiah 53:5, *"by whose stripes you were healed."* I have heard it said by some that this Scripture was not talking about physical healing, but "spiritual" healing.

As a matter of fact, not only have I heard that said, but the commentary in my *New King James Study Bible* also says this![6] Yet, if you read Matthew 8:16-17 you will see that this interpretation is wrong:

"When evening had come, they brought to Him many who were demon-possessed. And He cast out the spirits with a word, and healed all who were sick, that it might be fulfilled which was spoken by Isaiah the prophet, saying:

'He Himself took our infirmities and bore our sicknesses.'"

In this passage, Matthew makes a direct reference to Isaiah 53:4 and clearly says that Jesus cast out demons and *healed* those that where physically *sick* in order to fulfill Isaiah 53:3-5.

It can't get clearer than that. Isaiah the prophet was speaking about a Messiah who would come to deliver us from—not only our sins—but also from the consequences of our sin, including sickness, disease and death!

END NOTES

1. *New Bible Dictionary* (Downers Grove, Illinois: Intervarsity Press, 1996), page 102.

2. ibid., 102.

3. Roberts Liardon, *John G. Lake on Healing,* (New Kensington, PA: Whitaker House, 2009), page153.

4. *The New Strong's Exhaustive Concordance of the Bible (Strongs #2643)*, (Nashville TN, Thomas Nelson Publishers, 1990), page 914.

5. Ibid., 89.

6. *The Nelsons Study Bible, New King James Version*, (Nashville, TN: Thomas Nelson Publishers, 1997), page 2121. (Study note for 1 Peter 2:24)

chapter six

Is it God's Will for Everyone to be Healed?

F. F. Bosworth, a famous faith healer from the early 1900's, once said that, "The knowledge of God's will must precede faith for that will to be done."[1]

In other words, it is impossible to have the faith it takes to see someone healed if you're not sure that it's Gods will for them to be healed.

Pretend you're standing in front of someone who has cancer, and they've asked you to pray for them, but you're not sure if it's God's will for them to be healed. Having this unsurety, you'll automatically lack the faith it takes to get the job done.

To be honest, this was a topic that I struggled with for years. If you had asked me this question back when

I was a newly saved Christian, I most likely would have answered, "No, it is not Gods will for everyone to be healed." A few years later, I would have answered, "I'm not sure if it's God's will for everyone to be healed." Now, after walking with the Lord for sixteen years, I would say that, "*Yes*, it is *always* Gods will for *everyone* to be healed." Interestingly, when I held the view that it was not always God's will to heal, I never saw anyone that I prayed for healed. Not one single person! It was only when I got the revelation that it is always God's will to heal that I started seeing people healed.

Four Reasons Why I Believe it is Always God's Will to Heal Everyone

1. God is a good God, who loves to give His children good gifts.

"Ask, and it will be given to you; seek, and you will find; knock, and it will be opened to you. For everyone who asks receives, and he who seeks finds, and to him who knocks it will be opened. Or what man is there among you who, if his son asks for bread, will give him a stone? Or if he asks for a fish, will he give him a serpent? If you then, being evil, know how to give good gifts to your children, how much more will your Father who is in heaven give good things to those who ask Him!" (Matthew 7:7-11).

Is it God's Will for Everyone to be Healed?

I once heard Curry Blake give this powerful illustration (This is my paraphrase):

If you have children this will be easy to imagine. If you don't have children imagine for a minute that you do.

One day, your child comes up to you and says, "I'm hungry. I know that you don't have any food, but if you did you would gladly give some to me." In this scenario, the parent's *ability* to feed the child is questioned, but not their willingness.

Now imagine a different scenario. One day your child comes to you and says, "I'm hungry. I know you have plenty of food in the house, but I'm not sure you are willing to give it to me." In this scenario, the parent's *willingness* to feed the child is questioned, but not their ability.

Which scenario would grieve you as a parent more? The scenario where your ability to feed your child is questioned? Or the scenario where your willingness to feed your child is questioned? Most people would feel more grieved if their child questioned their *willingness* to feed them, rather than their ability to do so.

Now imagine another scenario. You come to God in prayer and say, "Lord, I know that you would heal Bob if you could. But I'm just not sure you can." In this scenario, God's *ability* to heal is questioned, but not His willingness.

Imagine a different scenario. You come to God in prayer and say, "Lord, I know that you can heal Bob if you want too. I'm just not sure that you want to." In this scenario Gods *willingness* to heal is questioned, but not His ability.

Which scenario do you think would grieve the heart of God more? Most people would select the scenario where Gods *willingness* to heal is questioned.

God (just like a parent) would much rather have you question His *ability* than His willingness. Yet, many Christians deeply grieve the heart of God by questioning his *willingness.*

I firmly believe that the best attitude to have and the attitude that blesses the heart of God the most is the attitude of, "God I know you *can* heal *AND* I know that you are *willing* to heal!"

My prayer is that after reading this chapter you will never again question God's ability to heal *or* His willingness to heal.

2. Healing is a Part of the Atonement

Though I dedicated the entire previous chapter to this topic, I want to share a few more Scriptures on this point.

First, consider Isaiah 53:3-5 which says:

"He is despised and rejected by men, A Man of sorrows and acquainted with grief. And we hid, as it were, our faces from Him; He was despised, and we did not esteem Him.

Surely He has borne our grief's And carried our sorrows; Yet we esteemed Him stricken, Smitten by God, and afflicted. But He was wounded for our transgressions, He was bruised for our iniquities; The chastisement for our peace was upon Him, And by His stripes we are healed."

This Scripture is a Messianic prophecy by the prophet Isaiah, given several hundred years before Jesus walked the earth.

In verse 4, the word "grief's"[2] could also be translated *"sickness,"* and the word "sorrows"[3] could be translated *"pain."* In other words verse 4 can be read:

*"Surely He has born our **sickness** and carried our **pain**."*

Beyond that, as mentioned in chapter five, Matthew 8:16-17 proves that this Scripture was not just referring to atonement for our spirits and the forgiveness of our sins. It also addresses the healing of our physical bodies.

A Detailed Look at the Crucifixion

We read about the crucifixion in the Bible, yet it's possible to forget what Jesus actually went through.

He experienced:

- Flogging: Jesus was tied naked to a post and struck over and over again in the back of the head, back, buttocks, and legs with a multi pronged whip with lead balls and sharp pieces of bones attached to it. The iron balls would cause deep contusions and the leather whip and sharp bones would cut deeply into the flesh, through the muscle tissue and even into the bone. The repeated strikes produced quivering ribbons of bleeding flesh. At times people would die from the flogging itself, due to shock or blood loss.

- Mocking & Beatings: Jesus endured severe mocking and physical abuse, before, during & after the flogging and also while He was on the cross.

- Crucifixion: Jesus was literally nailed to the cross with 7 inch long iron spikes driven through both of His wrists and feet. Victims of the cross hung there naked for hours or sometimes even days, before they would die. Insects would come and burrow into their torn flesh. Birds of prey would at times come and peck at their bodies, as people continued to mock them. The cross was designed as the ultimate torture device. The pain and humiliation the victims of the cross went through was slow and agonizing. In fact, the word "excruciating" comes from the Latin word "to crucify." When it was all said and done, when people were crucified they usually died of suffocation (due to the way their bodies hung), heart failure, or pure shock.[4]

When I read Isaiah 53:5, I can't help but think of the incredible price Jesus paid for our physical healing. Jesus wants you healed even more than you want to be healed! And He wants others to be healed, too. Every time I minister the gospel or pray for the sick, I think about the high price He paid. My heart's cry—just like the Moravians in the 1700's—is, "To win for the lamb the reward of His sufferings."[5]

Psalm 103:2-3 is another powerful Scripture that shows us two benefits of the atonement:

> "Let all that I am praise the Lord; may I never forget the good things he does for me. He forgives all my sins and **heals all my diseases.**" (NLT)

Bill Johnson says, "Sickness is to the body, what sin is to the soul."[6] Jesus paid a high price for our sins, but

He also paid a high price for the healing of our physical bodies.

So far we have seen how the atonement was for the physical body and the spirit, but did you know that the atonement was also for the soul (mind, will & emotions)?

Let's take a look at Leviticus 17:11:

*"For the life of the flesh is in the blood, and I have given it to you upon the altar to make atonement for your **souls**; for it is the blood that makes atonement for the **soul**."*

God's desire is for us to be made whole—body, soul and spirit. Since being saved in August of 1999, I couldn't tell you how many people I have seen saved (forgiven of their sins— Spirit), physically healed (Body), *AND* delivered from fear, anxiety, depression, bi-polar disorder and other mental disorders (Soul). Salvation is not just for the spirit, but also for the body and soul of a person!

Let's also take a look at 1 Timothy 2:1-4:

"Therefore I exhort first of all that supplications, prayers, intercessions, and giving of thanks be made for all men, for kings and all who are in authority, that we may lead a quiet and peaceable life in all godliness and reverence. For this is good and acceptable in the sight of God our

Savior, **who desires all men to be saved** *and to come to the knowledge of the truth."*

This Scripture makes it clear that it is God's desire that all men be saved. Remember, the Greek word for saved is the word "sozo," meaning to have eternal life, to be healed physically, to be delivered, protected and set free. It means to be made whole body, soul and spirit.

It is indeed God's will for everyone to be physically healed of sickness, disease and injury. The Bible has so much to say on the topic of God's will. Let's take a further look.

3. Sickness is a work of the enemy and Jesus came to destroy the works of the enemy.

"God anointed Jesus of Nazareth with the Holy Spirit and with power, who went about doing good and healing all who were **oppressed by the devil,** *for God was with Him."* (Acts 10:38).

Jesus viewed sickness as *oppression* from the *enemy*.

"For this purpose the Son of God was manifested, that He might **destroy the works of the devil"** (1 John 3:8).

If Jesus had a personal mission statement, this was it. The reason why Jesus came to this earth was to *destroy the works of the devil.* One of those works is sickness and disease.

> *"The thief does not come except to steal, and to kill, and to destroy. I have come that they may have life, and that they may have it more abundantly"* (John 10:10).

The devil is the one who came to steal, kill and destroy. Jesus is the one who came to give life, and life abundantly!

It's sad to say, but some Christians believe the opposite. Some Christians believe that God gives sickness and disease in order to get our attention, make us "better" people, or to teach us something. Often, these same people say that healing is not for today. They say it passed away when the last Apostles died. Because of this, they say if someone is healed, it must be a work of the devil! This couldn't be further from the truth. God is good and the devil is bad. The devil came to steal, kill and destroy. Jesus came to give abundant life. Can you learn something from being sick? Sure you can. But that doesn't mean that it was God who made you sick. It simply means that God can work all things together for the good of those who love Him (Romans 8:28).

4. When Jesus' will to heal was questioned, Jesus answered, "Yes, I am willing, be healed."

> *"And it happened when He was in a certain city, that behold, a man who was full of leprosy saw*

Jesus; and he fell on his face and implored Him, saying, "Lord, if You are willing, You can make me clean."

*Then He put out His hand and touched him, saying, "**I am willing**; be cleansed." Immediately the leprosy left him"* (Luke 5:12-13).

If it wasn't *always* God's will to heal, you would think that there would be at least one story in the gospels were Jesus said to someone, "No, I can't heal you because it is not God's will." But you never see that. As a matter of fact, there are many things you never hear Jesus say about healing. Let me give you just a few:

"Sorry, I can't heal you because you have too much bitterness in your life."

"Sorry, I can't heal you because it's not God's will." (As stated above)

"Sorry, I can't heal you because it's not God's timing."

"Sorry, I can't heal you because God's trying to teach you a lesson."

"Sorry, I can't heal you because you're harboring unforgiveness."

"Sorry, I can't heal you because (fill in the blank)."

Not only do we never hear Jesus say any of these things, we never hear the Apostles say any of these things in the book of Acts, either. If Jesus didn't say these things, and the Apostles didn't say these, why do we say these things? When we speak this way we are actually putting limitations on God.

Yet, I hear people list these as reasons as to why people aren't getting healed. The fact of the matter is, none of these are Biblical. As Curry Blake once said, "The only thing that can hinder healing is the belief that there are things that can hinder healing."[7]

Jesus never gave excuses as to why He could not heal someone. Instead, you see over and over again, the phrase, "And Jesus healed them *ALL!*" You never read, "And Jesus healed some of them." or "And Jesus healed a few of them." Every time it says, "And Jesus healed them *ALL!*"

So this begs the question: "If it is God's will for everyone to be healed, then why isn't everyone healed when we pray for them?" Let's read 2 Peter 3:9:

"The Lord is not slack concerning His promise, as some count slackness, but is longsuffering toward us, not willing that any should perish but that all should come to repentance."

Is it God's will for everyone to be saved (have eternal life)? Yes! The Scripture above makes that very clear. But will everyone be saved? No. Scripture also makes it clear that some will refuse to receive Him. So God's will is not always done here on earth. But that doesn't mean that it's not always God's will to heal and to save.

Think about this for a minute. Just because you pray for someone and they're not healed, *does not* mean that it wasn't Gods will for them to be healed. Yet, this is the exact conclusion so many have come to. We pray for someone's healing, and when they are not healed, we conclude that God doesn't want it to happen.

We have to be extremely careful that we don't build our doctrines on personal experience. Instead, we must base our doctrine on Scripture alone, in spite of what seems to us (at the time) to be a contradiction.

To further illustrate my point, let's look at Matthew 17:14-20:

"And when they (Jesus and His twelve disciples) had come to the multitude, a man came to Him (Jesus), kneeling down to Him and saying, "Lord, have mercy on my son, for he is an epileptic and suffers severely; for he often falls into the fire and often into the water. So I brought him to Your disciples, but they could not cure him."

Pretend for a minute that this story ended here. Many of us would be tempted to believe that the reason why the disciples could not heal the boy was because it wasn't God's will for the boy to be healed. After all, if it was God's will for this boy to be healed, then he would have been healed when the disciples prayed for him.

Let's read the rest of the story.

"Then Jesus answered and said, "O faithless and perverse generation, how long shall I be with you? How long shall I bear with you? Bring him here to Me." And Jesus rebuked the demon, and it came out of him; and the child was cured from that very hour.

Then the disciples came to Jesus privately and said, "Why could we not cast it out?"

So Jesus said to them, "Because of your unbelief; for assuredly, I say to you, if you have faith as a mustard seed, you will say to this mountain, 'Move from here to there,' and it will move; and nothing will be impossible for you."

It *was* God's will to heal this boy. The problem wasn't with God or His willingness to heal. The problem was with the disciples and their lack of faith.

When teaching this subject I get asked quite frequently, "whom do you blame if you pray for someone and they aren't healed?" Too many people want to blame God (for His lack of willingness or ability to heal) or the person they are praying for (for their lack of faith). But I don't see either as Biblical. I respond by telling them that I never blame the sick person for not getting healed because if I am the one praying for them I am the one who should have the faith. I also never blame God because I believe it is always God's will to heal everyone. Instead I focus on my responsibility to grow in this gifting and walk in faith.

It does take some faith to lay hands on the sick and see them healed. The good news is that it does not take great faith. It just takes a little faith. Matthew 17:20 says that all you need is faith the size of a mustard seed and you can speak to your mountain and your mountain will be removed.

It all goes back to the quote by F. F. Bosworth at the beginning of the chapter. A huge part of the battle is simply knowing that *it is* God's will for the person you are praying for to be healed. If you know that, chances are you will have the faith it takes to get the job done.

END NOTES

1. F.F. Bosworth, *Christ the Healer* (Grand Rapids, MI: Chosen Books, 2008), page 176.

2. *The New Strong's Exhaustive Concordance of the Bible (Strongs #2483)*, (Nashville, TN: Thomas Nelson Publishers, 1990), page 436.

3. *The New Strong's Exhaustive Concordance of the Bible (Strongs #4341)*, (Nashville, TN: Thomas Nelson Publishers, 1990), page 997.

4. www.frugalsites.net/Jesus/scourging.htm. (This site is currently under construction as of April 28, 2016.)

5. http://www.globaltribesoutreach.org/articlesmoravian. Accessed April 28, 2016.

6. Bill Johnson, *When Heaven Invades Earth* (Shippensburg, PA: Destiny Image Publishers Inc., 2003), page 31.

7. http://www.divinerevelations.info/documents/healing/jgl/jgl_ministries.htm. Accessed April 28, 2016.

chapter seven

The Role of the Believer vs. The Role of the Five-Fold Minister

First of all, I want to point out that throughout this book you will see that I use certain Scriptures multiple times. Some times this is done in order to re-emphasize important points. Other times, this is done because there are multiple points I want to make using the same Scripture.

Secondly, I'm including this chapter in the book to further solidify the fact that healing the sick is something *every* believer is called to do.

In his book "The Coming Revival," Dr. Bill Bright quotes a statistic that says "Only *two percent* of believers in America regularly share their faith in Christ with others."[1] This is a startling statistic in light of the fact that *one hundred percent* of believers are called to share the gospel regularly (Mark 16:15-18)! I am willing to bet that far less than two percent of Christians in America see the sick healed regularly.

It's sad to say but it has become so rare to find believers in the church who actually fulfill the role of a believer (sharing the gospel, casting out demons and healing the sick) that any believer who shares the gospel regularly is called an "evangelist" and any believer who has had any success casting out demons or healing the sick is told they have a "special gifting, calling or anointing". The fact is, that sharing the gospel, casting out demons and healing the sick is supposed to be a normal part of every believers day to day life! As I state in a previous chapter these things are not just for a select few "Christian superstars" or people in full time ministry. They are for *every* believer!

At this point in history there are over 7 billion people living on this planet. There are approximately 2 billion Christians on the planet, which means there are about 5 billion people living on this planet that do not yet know Christ as their Savior. It's going to take the entire body of Christ to reach all people, not just the evangelists or other 5-fold ministers. In this chapter, I'm going to clearly define the role of the believer and the role of the 5-fold minister. There is a lot of confusion on this topic. This has led many believers to rely on a small portion of the body of Christ to do the vast majority of world evangelism.

THE CALLING OF THE BELIEVER

Mark 16:15-18 says:

"And He said to them, 'Go into all the world and preach the gospel to every creature. He who believes and is baptized will be saved; but he who does not believe will be condemned. **And these signs will follow those who believe***: In My name they will cast out demons; they will speak with new tongues; they will take up serpents; and if they drink anything deadly, it will by no means hurt them; they will lay hands on the sick, and they will recover.'"*

In this passage, Jesus specifically says that every one who *believes* is called to:

- Preach the gospel.
- Cast out demons.
- Heal the sick.

2 Corinthians 5:17-21 says:

"Therefore, if anyone is in Christ, he is a new creation; old things have passed away; behold, all things have become new. Now all things are of God, who has reconciled us to Himself through

Jesus Christ, and has given us the **ministry** *of reconciliation, that is, that God was in Christ reconciling the world to Himself, not imputing their trespasses to them,* **and has committed to us the word of reconciliation. Now then, we are ambassadors for Christ, as though God were pleading through us: we implore you on Christ's behalf, be reconciled to God.** *For He made Him who knew no sin to be sin for us, that we might become the righteousness of God in Him."*

Are you in Christ? Have you been reconciled to God? If so, *you are called to the ministry!* That's right. *Every believer* is called to the ministry! "What ministry?" you may ask, the ministry of reconciliation. Curry Blake explains the ministry of reconciliation this way. He says that its:

- Reconciling people's bodies back to God through divine *healing*

- Reconciling people's souls back to God through *deliverance*

- Reconciling people's spirits back to God through *salvation*[2]

In other words, believers are *all* called to bring people into the *entire* salvation experience. Remember the Greek word for "saved"—*sozo?* Sozo, does not only mean the redemption of a person's spirit, but of their bodies and souls as well.

Every believer is called to this ministry of reconciliation. Every believer is called to heal the sick. Every believer is called to deliver the captives. Every believer is called to share the gospel.

John 14:12 says:

*"Most assuredly, I say to you, **he who believes in Me**, the works that I do he will do also; and greater works than these he will do, because I go to My Father."*

Jesus says that those who *believe* in Him will do the *same* things He did. Even greater things than He did! In John 8:12, Jesus calls Himself the light of the world. In Matthew 5:14-16, He also calls those who *believe* in Him the light of the world:

*"**You** are the light of the world. A city that is set on a hill cannot be hidden. Nor do they light a lamp and put it under a basket, but on a lampstand, and it gives light to all who are in the house. Let **your** light so shine before men, that they may see **your** good works and glorify **your** Father in heaven."*

Are you starting to see it? We are called to do the *same* works Jesus did. Jesus called Himself the light of the world, and then called those who *believe* in Him the light of the world. Who is the "we" He is referring too? The "we" is simply *anyone who believes in Jesus Christ!* But the comparisons don't end there.

> *"So Jesus said to them again, "Peace to you! As the Father has sent Me, I also send you"* (John 20:21).

In this passage Jesus tells His disciples that He is sending them out on the same mission that the Father sent Him on. What mission was that? It was the mission of destroying the works of the devil (1 John 3:8) and reconciling people (body, soul & spirit) back to God (2 Corinthians 5:17-21) through healing the sick, casting out demons and sharing the good news (Mark 16:15-18).

Some may argue that in the context of John chapter 20, Jesus was specifically commissioning the twelve disciples, and that this Scripture was not talking about us. This would be a fair point to make. However, just a few chapters before, Jesus makes the same statement. It is very clear that Jesus is talking not *just* to His twelve disciples but to *every* believer that would come after them as well. This includes you and me!

> *"As You sent Me into the world, I also have sent them into the world. And for their sakes I sanctify Myself, that they also may be sanctified by the truth."* *"I do not pray for these alone (His twelve disciples), but also for those who will believe in Me through their word (you and me);"* (John 17:18-20).

Over the years, I have seen many people saved, healed and delivered. Some have said, "Well, you have a special calling and anointing to be an evangelist." I want to make it clear that I haven't seen one person saved, healed or delivered because I have a special anointing or because I am an evangelist. The reason I have seen many people saved, healed and set free is because I am a *believer* in Jesus Christ who decided to step out!

Likewise, the apostles didn't do all those amazing things we read about in the book of Acts because they were apostles, but because they were *believers* in Jesus Christ.

You can take any modern day Five-fold minister and say the same thing. Let's take Heidi Baker, Reinhard Bonnke and Bill Johnson, for example. They don't see people healed, saved and set free because of any special anointing, gifting, or calling. They see many people touched simply because they are *believers* who decided to step out and go after it!

I know these are some pretty radical statements I'm making. It may be hard for some to wrap their minds around this. I also know that it begs the question, "So what is the five-fold minister for?"

The Calling of The Five-Fold Minister

The calling, or job description of the five-fold minister is found in Ephesians 4:11-13. Let's read:

*"And He Himself gave some to be **apostles**, some **prophets**, some **evangelists**, and some **pastors** and **teachers**, for the equipping of the saints for the work of ministry, for the edifying of the body of Christ, till we all come to the unity of the faith and of the knowledge of the Son of God, to a perfect man, to the measure of the stature of the fullness of Christ;"*

Is there anything in these verses about healing the sick, casting out demons or sharing the gospel? No. Why not? Because that's the role of the believer, not the five-fold minister. Do five-fold ministers heal the sick, cast out demons and share the gospel? Yes they do. But they do that because they are believers, not because they are a pastor, teacher, prophet, evangelist or an apostle.

The role of the five-fold minister according to Ephesians 4:11-13 is to:

- Build up the body of Christ

- Help the body of Christ to grow and look more like Jesus

- Equip the body of Christ for the work of *ministry*

What ministry you ask? The ministry of reconciliation—which is healing the sick, casting out demons and sharing the gospel.

Believers need to understand that they have just as much power, anointing *and responsibility* to heal the sick, cast out demons and share the gospel as any five-fold minister. You need to realize that the All-Powerful One and the Anointed One lives inside of you just as much as He lives inside of Heidi Baker, Reinhard Bonnke, Bill Johnson, the apostle Paul, or any other five-fold minister! The only difference is that the five-fold minister has the *added* responsibility to teach and equip you for the work of the ministry and help you grow up to look more like Jesus.

Top Two Reasons Why Believers Don't Share the Gospel

Over the years, I have come to learn what I believe to be the top two reasons why believers don't share the gospel regularly.

1. Fear.

2. Lack of training.

As five-fold ministers, we need to do a much better job of training believers how to share the gospel, cast out demons, and heal the sick. We also need to help believers overcome their fear of stepping out by providing them safe opportunities to do so. They need to walk with others who have experienced doing these things and have seen them in action. This is a desperate need in the Church today!

JOB DESCRIPTIONS:
Every Believer vs. The Five-Fold Minister

To summarize what I am saying, let's look at this side by side comparison of what I will call the "job description" of *every believer* vs. the "job description" of the five-fold minister (apostle, prophet, evangelist, pastor & teacher)

Every Believer – Mark 16:15-18

- Preach the gospel
- Cast out demons
- Heal the sick

The Five-Fold Minister – Ephesians 4:11-13

- Build up the body of Christ
- Help the body of Christ to grow up and look more like Jesus
- Equip the body of Christ for the work of *ministry*

As Believers, the Five-fold minister also has the responsibility to:

- Preach the gospel
- Cast out demons
- Heal the sick

In closing, I will give you one final illustration. I do a lot of street evangelism in Harrisburg, Pennsylvania. I also teach at various ministry schools and churches. When I am on the streets of Harrisburg sharing the gospel, healing the sick, and setting captives free, I am fulfilling my role as a believer. When I am teaching in a ministry school or Church, I am fulfilling my role as a five-fold minister (evangelist).

The bottom line is that Jesus has called *ALL believers* to fulfill the great commission (Mark 16:15-18). He has called *EVERY believer* to preach the gospel, heal the sick and set the captives free!

END NOTES

1. Dr. Bill Bright, *The Coming Revival* (New Life Publications, 1995), page 65.

2. http://www.divinerevelations.info/documents/healing/jgl/jgl_ministries.htm. Accessed April 28, 2016.

chapter eight

Seeing People Through the Eyes of Christ

This is the heart behind it all. This is our motivation. This is why we do what we do. I believe in the great commission. I'm all about Mark 16:15-18 and Matthew 28:18-20. In fact I've been sharing Mark 16:15-18 throughout this entire book. But really, this whole thing is less about the great commission and more about the great commandment.

The Great Commandment

One day, Jesus was having a discussion with some Pharisees and Sadducees. One of them asked Him what the greatest commandment was. Jesus said to them:

> *"'You shall love the L*ORD *your God with all your heart, with all your soul, and with all your mind.' This is the first and great commandment. And the second is like it: 'You shall love your neighbor as yourself'"* (Matthew 22:37-39).

This whole thing is all about love. If you love God and love other people, you won't be able to resist reaching out to others. It will come so naturally to you that you won't be able to not reach out.

As much as the Church needs a revelation that they *can* heal the sick, they need a revolution of love in their lives. It's my prayer that this chapter will spark, not only a deeper love for God within you, but also a greater love and compassion for people.

Love and Compassion

It's hard for me to pick my favorite Scripture, because there are so many good ones. But if I had to pick just one, perhaps Matthew 9:35-38 would be it. This is a Scripture the Lord has brought to my attention over and over again, since the day I was born again 16 years ago. It's been a constant reminder to me of why I do what I do. Each time I read it, I am reminded of how much our Savior loves us. I'm overwhelmed with a sense of love and compassion for others.

> *"Then Jesus went about all the cities and villages, teaching in their synagogues, preaching*

the gospel of the kingdom, and healing every sickness and every disease among the people. But when He saw the multitudes, He was moved with compassion for them, because they were weary and scattered, like sheep having no shepherd. Then He said to His disciples, 'The harvest truly is plentiful, but the laborers are few. Therefore pray the Lord of the harvest to send out laborers into His harvest.'"

Many years ago (2002), as a freshman in Bible school, my grandmother, Maxine Lewis, gave me a tape to listen to. The tape was from Moody Bible Institute, which was the Bible school she had attended and where she met my grandfather. Each year Moody has a conference called "Founders Week." She gave me a tape by Crawford Loritts called, "Recapturing Our Sense of Missions."

At this time, I had been saved for just a little over two years and had an unquenchable passion to share my faith with others (as I still do). Listening to this tape made a great impact on my life. It is without a doubt the most powerful sermon on evangelism I have ever heard. It is so powerful that, over the past 13 years, I have listened to this tape dozens of times. Each time, without fail, I am moved to tears. This tape means so much to me that I took the time to transcribe this sermon! I know that tapes don't last forever. So when this tape wears out (which its already starting to do) I will at least have the sermon in written form to read. I want to share with you just one quote from this tape. Crawford Loritts made this point from Matthew 9:36:

> "Seeing He (Jesus) *felt*. Seeing He *felt*. Not, seeing He strategized. Not seeing He analyzed. Not seeing He criticized. Not seeing He denounced! But seeing He *felt* compassion. The Greek word for compassion is the word bowels. I don't mean to be gross, but I think that captures the intensity of the moment more than just the word compassion. You know how your stomach *felt* when you saw those planes flying into the twin towers? You know how your stomach *felt* when you saw those people walking down the streets of Manhattan holding pictures of loved ones? That's the idea here, when Jesus saw the condition of the multitudes, *His heart hurt for them.*"[1]

Author and speaker Brennan Manning says this:

> "When you read in the gospels that Jesus was moved with compassion, it is saying that His gut was wrenched, His heart torn open, the most vulnerable part of His being laid bare. The ground of all being shook, the source of all life trembled, the heart of all love burst open and the unfathomable depths of relentless tenderness was laid bare."[2]

Yes, people can be messed up. It's all too easy for us to look at them and be critical. It's easy for us to look at them and judge. Jesus wasn't saying that these people weren't guilty of sin. But Jesus saw that there were other things and other people that contributed to the mess their lives had become. Sure, these people had sinned, but they had also been sinned against.

It's like a child who was abused, only to grow up and continue the cycle of abuse. Or, the child whose only role model is a parent who is a drug or alcohol addict. They grow up to be just like their parents. It's too easy for us to look at the drunk, homeless man on the street and think, "Well, if he'd only stop drinking and get a job!" It's so easy to judge people, when we don't know the whole story.

I've been doing ministry in the inner city for fourteen years. I've done homeless ministry, street ministry (both in Rochester, New York and Harrisburg, Pennsylvania), and children's ministry at an inner city Church. I was a youth pastor in Rochester, New York, and I was the program director at a Christian after school program in Harrisburg, Pennsylvania for seven years. In 2011, I started a ministry called Sent Ones, in Harrisburg. We do a lot of street ministry, feed the hungry, and disciple those we meet during our outreaches. Over the years, I've had certain encounters with people that I will never forget. Each one of these encounters has taught me priceless life lessons.

Several years ago, as the program director at Center for Champions, I had one of these life-changing encounters. The Church we rented space from was huge, but the congregation was small. It was a tiny Spanish Church made up of about thirty people. Though small in number, this Church did great things for the community of South Allison Hill. Handing out groceries to people in need was one of the many things they did. A couple times a week, people would be lined up around the building to receive bags of food. Often, while at work, I would run into this homeless man named David. Amazingly, David was not there to receive the grocery bags of food, but to help the Church hand out the food. After the outreach was over, I would often run into David while he was breaking down cardboard boxes to take out to the trash.

I would see David several times each week. And every time I saw him, I would make a point to stop and talk to him. David's first language was Spanish. He did speak English, but it was very broken. I would understand a few words out of each sentence he spoke and piece together what he was saying. David was dirty and always had the potent smell of alcohol on his breath. But this man had a sweet spirit about him. After every conversation, he would always ask me to pray for him.

One day, after David had left the outreach, the pastor of the Church came to me and asked me if I new David's story? I had built a good relationship with David over the past couple years, but I didn't know much about his personal life. The pastor went on to tell me all about David's life and how he became homeless.

The pastor said that David was once a well-respected member of the community. David had a job, he had a house and he had a wife and a couple of children. One day, several years ago, his wife and children died in a tragic car accident. David never had a drug or alcohol problem before, but the pain was too much for him to bear. During this tragic time, David (for the first time in his life) turned to alcohol to numb the pain. Over the course of time, David became addicted to alcohol. This led to him losing his job, losing his house. As a result, he ended up homeless on the streets of Harrisburg.

The thing that motivated Jesus to reach the multitudes was His love and compassion for them. Jesus saw the "David's" of this world as confused and helpless, like sheep who have no shepherd. His love and compassion is what motivated Jesus to do the things He did.

I encourage you to spend some time meditating on Matthew 9:35-38. Do a study on the word compassion. Let it sink into your spirit and let it move you into action. There's no time to lose. Matthew 9:38 is as true today as it was 2,000 years ago. The harvest is truly great. There are people all around us that are ripe and ready to receive the good news. But there's a worker problem. The enemy has deceived the body of Christ into thinking that sharing the good news is someone else's job. And because we have bought into this lie, the crops are dying on the field.

END NOTES

1. Crawford Loritts, *Recapturing Our Sense of Missions* (820 N. La Salle Blvd. Chicago, IL: Moody Cassette Ministry, 2002) Cassette Tape, Founder's Week.

2. http://www.keylife.org/articles/brennan-manning-on-gods-love. Accessed April 28, 2016.

chapter nine

Paul's Thorn in the Flesh

I teach on the subject of healing frequently. When I teach there are a few questions that almost always come up. In these last three chapters, I will be answering some of the most common questions I've been asked about healing.

Paul's Thorn

I remember an encounter I had with a fellow Christian several years ago. I was leading an outreach in the inner city of Harrisburg. We were serving free hot dogs and drinks, giving out free Bibles, and offering prayer to people. A man came up for some free food. I had seen this man before. He always used crutches to help him walk. It was obvious that he had some sort of chronic issue with his legs. I came up to him and asked him if I could pray for his legs. His answer shocked me. He scowled at me and, in a harsh tone of voice, yelled, "This is my thorn in the flesh!" He went on to tell me how God had given him this disability to humble him. I tried reasoning with him, but he just turned and walked away.

Over the years, I have heard many Christians claim to have "Paul's thorn." They believe that God gave them their illness for one reason or another. This is exactly what the enemy would like us to think! He would like us to blame God for our illness instead of him! The truth is, Paul's thorn was not given to him by God, and it was not sickness or disease. If Paul's thorn was not given to him by God then, who gave it to him? And if Paul's thorn was not sickness or disease, what was it? Let's read 2 Corinthians 12:7-10 to find out:

*"And lest I (Paul) should be exalted above measure by the abundance of the revelations, a thorn in the flesh was given to me, a **messenger** of **Satan** to buffet me, lest I be exalted above measure. Concerning this thing I pleaded with the Lord three times that it might depart from me. And He said to me, "My grace is sufficient for you, for My strength is made perfect in weakness." Therefore most gladly I will rather boast in my infirmities, that the power of Christ may rest upon me. Therefore I take pleasure in infirmities, in reproaches, in needs, in **persecutions**, in distresses, for Christ's sake. For when I am weak, then I am strong."*

In this passage Paul tells us what his thorn was and who gave it to him. Paul's thorn was a *"messenger"* that was sent by *"Satan"* (not God). In other words, Paul's thorn was a person or group of people. This is consistent with the rest of Scripture. Everywhere in Scripture where the term "thorn in the flesh" is used it speaks of a person or a group of people that is coming against another person or group of people. The term "thorn in the flesh" is *never* used in the Bible to describe sickness or disease. Let me give you two examples:

*"Now the Lord spoke to Moses in the plains of Moab by the Jordan, across from Jericho, saying, "Speak to the children of Israel, and say to them: 'When you have crossed the Jordan into the land of Canaan, then you shall drive out all the inhabitants of the land from before you, destroy all their engraved stones, destroy all their molded images, and demolish all their high places; you shall dispossess the inhabitants of the land and dwell in it, for I have given you the land to possess. And you shall divide the land by lot as an inheritance among your families; to the larger you shall give a larger inheritance, and to the smaller you shall give a smaller inheritance; there everyone's inheritance shall be whatever falls to him by lot. You shall inherit according to the tribes of your fathers. But if you do not drive out the **inhabitants** of the land from before you, then it shall be that **those whom you let remain***

*shall be irritants in your eyes and **thorns in your sides**, and they shall harass you in the land where you dwell"* (Numbers 33:50-55).

In this passage, God gives Moses instructions for the conquest of Canaan. In verse 55, God tells Moses that if he failed to drive out the inhabitants of the land of Canaan, the *people* of Canaan would become a *"thorn in your side."* This thorn had nothing to do with sickness or disease. The thorn mentioned in this passage was a group of people. Let's look at another example:

"Now it came to pass, a long time after the Lord had given rest to Israel from all their enemies round about, that Joshua was old, advanced in age. And Joshua called for all Israel, for their elders, for their heads, for their judges, and for their officers, and said to them:

"I am old, advanced in age. You have seen all that the Lord your God has done to all these nations because of you, for the Lord your God is He who has fought for you. See, I have divided to you by lot these nations that remain, to be an inheritance for your tribes, from the Jordan, with all the nations that I have cut off, as far as the Great Sea westward. And the Lord your God will expel them from before you and drive them out of your sight. So you shall possess their land, as the Lord your God promised you. Therefore be very courageous to keep and to do all that is

written in the Book of the Law of Moses, lest you turn aside from it to the right hand or to the left, and lest you go among these nations, these who remain among you. You shall not make mention of the name of their gods, nor cause anyone to swear by them; you shall not serve them nor bow down to them, but you shall hold fast to the Lord your God, as you have done to this day. For the Lord has driven out from before you great and strong nations; but as for you, no one has been able to stand against you to this day. One man of you shall chase a thousand, for the Lord your God is He who fights for you, as He promised you. Therefore take careful heed to yourselves, that you love the Lord your God. Or else, if indeed you do go back, and cling to the remnant of these nations—these that remain among you—and make marriages with them, and go in to them and they to you, know for certain that the Lord your God will no longer drive out these nations from before you. But they shall be snares and traps to you, and scourges on your sides and **thorns in your eyes**, *until you perish from this good land which the Lord your God has given you"* (Joshua 23:1-13).

In this passage, Joshua gives his farewell address. In this address Joshua gives a stern warning to the people of Israel. He warns the people that if they do not remain completely separated from the people of the nations they just conquered that these *people* would become *"thorns in their eyes."* Again, the "thorn" had nothing to do with sickness or disease. The thorn in this passage was a group of *people*.

The Greek word translated "messenger" in 2 Corinthians 12:7 is the word "angelos."[1] This Greek word "angelos" is mentioned 188 times in the New Testament. 181 times it is translated "angel" and 7 times it is translated "messenger" (Example: 2 Corinthians 12:7). This word always refers to a person or a being (like an angel). Not one time does it ever refer to sickness or disease.

So, if Paul's thorn in the flesh was not sickness or disease, what was it? Let's take a look at a few more Scriptures:

"Now there was a certain disciple at Damascus named Ananias; and to him the Lord said in a vision, "Ananias."

And he said, "Here I am, Lord."

So the Lord said to him, "Arise and go to the street called Straight, and inquire at the house of Judas for one called Saul of Tarsus, for behold, he is praying. And in a vision he has seen a man named Ananias coming in and putting his hand on him, so that he might receive his sight."

Then Ananias answered, "Lord, I have heard from many about this man, how much harm he has done to Your saints in Jerusalem. And here he has authority from the chief priests to bind all who call on Your name."

*But the Lord said to him, "Go, for he is a chosen vessel of Mine to bear My name before Gentiles, kings, and the children of Israel. **For I will show him how many things he must suffer for My name's sake.**"*

And Ananias went his way and entered the house; and laying his hands on him he said, "Brother Saul, the Lord Jesus, who appeared to you on the road as you came, has sent me that you may receive your sight and be filled with the Holy Spirit." Immediately there fell from his eyes something like scales, and he received his sight at once; and he arose and was baptized.

So when he had received food, he was strengthened. Then Saul spent some days with the disciples at Damascus" (Acts 9:10-19).

What things did Paul suffer for spreading the gospel? The Apostle Paul tells us himself:

"Instead, I sometimes think God has put us apostles on display, like prisoners of war at the end of a victor's parade, condemned to die. We have become a spectacle to the entire world—to people and angels alike. Our dedication to Christ makes us look like fools, but you claim to

*be so wise in Christ! We are weak, but you are so powerful! You are honored, but we are ridiculed. Even now we go **hungry and thirsty**, and we **don't have enough clothes to keep warm**. We are often **beaten** and **have no home**. We work wearily with our own hands to earn our living. We bless those who curse us. We are patient with those who **abuse** us. We appeal gently when evil things are said about us. Yet we are **treated like the world's garbage**, like everybody's trash—right up to the present moment"* (1 Corinthians 4:9-13, NLT).

*"Are they Hebrews? So am I. Are they Israelites? So am I. Are they descendants of Abraham? So am I. Are they servants of Christ? I know I sound like a madman, but I have served him far more! I have worked harder, been put in **prison** more often, been **whipped times without number**, and **faced death** again and again. **Five different times the Jewish leaders gave me thirty-nine lashes.** Three times I was **beaten with rods**. Once I was **stoned**. Three times I was **shipwrecked**. Once **I spent a whole night and a day adrift at sea**. I have traveled on many long journeys. I have **faced danger from rivers and from robbers**. **I have faced danger from my own people, the Jews, as well as from the Gentiles.** I have faced danger in the cities, in the deserts, and on the seas. And I have faced danger from*

*men who claim to be believers but are not. I have worked hard and long, enduring many **sleepless nights**. I have been **hungry** and **thirsty** and have often **gone without food**. I have **shivered in the cold, without enough clothing** to keep me warm"* (2 Corinthians 11:22-27, NLT).

The Apostle Paul suffered much for the sake of the gospel. He suffered hunger, thirst, lack of clothing, was shipwrecked, spent a whole night and day adrift at sea, spent many sleepless nights, and was homeless. He also faced death, was imprisoned, whipped multiple times, beaten with rods, and stoned. The one thing you *don't* find on this list is any mention of suffering from sickness or disease.

Paul's thorn in the flesh was the *persecution* he faced for preaching the gospel, not sickness or disease. Some of you may be thinking, "What about the Scripture where the Galatians told Paul, 'how we wish we could gouge out our eyes and give them to you'?" (Galatians 4:15) Many people use this Scripture to support the theory that Paul had some sort of eye disease. The fact of the matter is that Paul had just come to Galatia directly after being stoned and left for dead. When they stoned people back then they would throw huge rocks at your head, face and every other part of your body with the purpose of killing you. When Paul went to Galatia he would have looked like a bloody mess. The Galatians where using a figure of speech much like we would today. Have you ever heard some one say to another person "I'd give my right arm for them!" Of course they don't mean it literally. It is a figure of speech.

I will end with one more Scripture:

"Behold, I send you out as sheep in the midst of wolves. Therefore be wise as serpents and harmless as doves. But beware of men, for they will deliver you up to councils and scourge you in their synagogues. You will be brought before governors and kings for My sake, as a testimony to them and to the Gentiles. But when they deliver you up, do not worry about how or what you should speak. For it will be given to you in that hour what you should speak; for it is not you who speak, but the Spirit of your Father who speaks in you.

"Now brother will deliver up brother to death, and a father his child; and children will rise up against parents and cause them to be put to death. And you will be hated by all for My name's sake. But he who endures to the end will be saved. When they persecute you in this city, flee to another. For assuredly, I say to you, you will not have gone through the cities of Israel before the Son of Man comes" (Matthew 10:16-23).

Jesus never promised us sickness and disease. He did, however, promise us persecution for spreading the gospel.

END NOTE

1. *The New Strongs Exhaustive Concordance of the Bible (Strongs #32)*, (Nashville TN: Thomas Nelson Publishers, 1990), page 702.

chapter ten

Do You Need Faith in Order to be Healed?

Many people believe that the sick person you are praying for has to have faith in order to be healed. Often times they say, "Jesus could not heal any sick people in His own home town because of their unbelief." When people say this, they are actually taking two different Scriptures, mixing them together and misquoting both of them. By doing this they form a doctrine that is completely unbiblical. Let's take a look at these two different Scriptures.

Mark 6:5 says:

*"Now He (Jesus) **could do no** mighty works there, except that He laid His hands on a few sick people and healed them."*

This Scripture seems to indicate that Jesus *could not do* mighty works in this town. Some people I talk to use this Scripture to back up their claims that the person being prayed for has to have faith in order to be healed. They say, "Look! Jesus *could not* heal the people in Mark 6:5 because of their unbelief." However, these same people seem to skip over an important detail. That is, that Jesus *did* heal a few sick people.

The second Scripture I want to look at is Matthew 13:58:

*"Now **He did not do** mighty works there because of their unbelief."*

Matthew's version seems to indicate that Jesus *chose not to* do many mighty works. However, the use of the word *"many"* seems to indicate that He did do some. In other words in spite of the people's unbelief Jesus *did* in fact perform some miracles and heal some sick people.

Why Did Jesus Limit the Amount of Mighty Works in His Own Hometown?

I've heard some people say that Jesus could have healed them, but because of their unbelief they didn't *come to Him* and request healing. I think this is a valid point and believe this certainly could have been a contributing factor. Especially seeing's that most of the people we see healed in the gospels are people who *came to Jesus*. But I also think that Wayne Jackson has a valid point, as well. He says:

> "The seeming problem is with Mark's expression *"He could not."* The Greek phraseology is "ouk edunato." This expression is an idiomatic manner of speaking occasionally employed in the New Testament to connote the idea that one, for some reason, *chooses not* to do something—though technically, he has the ability to do it. Consider these examples.
>
> In one of his epistles, the apostle John writes:
>
> "Whosoever is begotten of God does no sin, because his (God's) seed abideth in him: and he cannot (ou dunamai) sin, because he is begotten of God" (1 John 3:9, ASV).
>
> The apostle is not suggesting that it is impossible for the child of God to sin (cf. 1 John 1:8-9; 2:1-2); rather, he is stating that when divine truth becomes resident in the heart, one will *choose* not to yield ourselves to a habitual, unrestrained life of sin. The term "cannot" is used in the sense of a moral imperative."[1]

In other words, it was not that Jesus COULD NOT do many miracles in His hometown. It was that He refrained from doing many miracles in His hometown. He *CHOSE* not to (Again, according to Mark 6:5, Jesus did heal a few people).

Often times we find the answer to our question when we read a Scripture in context. Look at Matthew 13:53-58:

> *"Now it came to pass, when Jesus had finished these parables, that He departed from there. When He had come to His own country, He taught them in their synagogue, so that they were astonished and said, "Where did this Man get this wisdom and these mighty works? Is this not the carpenter's son? Is not His mother called Mary? And His brothers James, Joses, [a] Simon, and Judas? And His sisters, are they not all with us? Where then did this Man get all these things?"* **So they were offended at Him.**
>
> *But Jesus said to them, "A prophet is not without honor except in his own country and in his own house." Now He did not do many mighty works there because of their unbelief."*

The people who lived in Jesus' hometown were offended at Him. It reminds me of the time when the Pharisees demanded a sign (miracle) from Jesus, and Jesus refused to give them one.

> *"A wicked and adulterous generation seeks after a sign, and no sign shall be given to it except the*

sign of the prophet[a] Jonah." And He left them and departed" (Matthew 16:4).

"Then the Pharisees came out and began to dispute with Him, seeking from Him a sign from heaven, testing Him. But He sighed deeply in His spirit, and said, "Why does this generation seek a sign? Assuredly, I say to you, no sign shall be given to this generation" (Mark 8:11-13).

Could Jesus have performed miracles in front of the Pharisees? Sure He could have. But because of the state of their hearts *He chose not to.*

An Atheist Healed

So, does the person you are praying for have to have faith in order to get healed? Let me tell you a story from one of my own experiences.

Several years ago, I had an encounter with an atheist. I stopped to talk to him because I noticed he was limping and wanted to pray for him.

I asked, "Why are you limping?"

He said, "When I was younger, I stepped on a nail, and ever since I've had pain in my foot, and I limp because of it."

After talking for a couple of minutes, he made it clear that he didn't believe in God and he didn't believe that he would be healed if I prayed for him.

I asked him, "What do you have to lose? Either I pray for you and nothing happens or I pray for you and you're healed. Worst case scenario you waste 30 seconds of time. Best case scenario, you walk away completely healed with no more pain and no more limp."

It took some convincing, but eventually he let me pray for him.

I knelt down and laid my hands on his foot and said, "Pain I command you to go. Foot be healed."

Before I could even stand up, he began to shout some expletives saying, "I can't believe it! My foot's totally pain free!

I encouraged him to test it out. As he walked around pain free, without a limp, he looked both confused and amazed. He was completely healed!

Since that time, I have seen a number of self-proclaimed atheists instantly and miraculously healed. Not one of these atheists had an ounce of faith to be healed, yet they were.

Jesus Raises a Man from the Dead

Let's read this story from Luke 7:11-17.

"Now it happened, the day after, that He went into a city called Nain; and many of His disciples went with Him, and a large crowd. And when He came near the gate of the city, behold, a dead

man was being carried out, the only son of his mother; and she was a widow. And a large crowd from the city was with her. When the Lord saw her, He had compassion on her and said to her, "Do not weep." Then He came and touched the open coffin, and those who carried him stood still. And He said, "Young man, I say to you, arise." So he who was dead sat up and began to speak. And He presented him to his mother.

Then fear came upon all, and they glorified God, saying, "A great prophet has risen up among us"; and, "God has visited His people." And this report about Him went throughout all Judea and all the surrounding region."

One simple question: Can a dead corpse have faith for healing? Of course not! If faith for healing was required by the one being prayed for then Jesus could have never raised the dead.

Does the Person You're Praying for Have to Have Faith in Order to be Healed?

Does the person you're praying for have to have faith in order to be healed? No, they do not. Faith is required (Matthew 17:20). But it can be the faith of the person who is being prayed for *or it can be the faith of the person who is doing the praying*. It can be either.

Just as a reminder, as I stated in chapter six, if the person I pray for is not healed I never blame them for their lack of faith. If I am the one praying then I should be the one who has the faith. Also, blaming the person you are praying for can be really hurtful to them. I also never blame God because I believe it is always His will to heal everyone. Instead I focus on my responsibility to grow in this gifting and walk in faith.

END NOTE

1. https://www.christiancourier.com/articles/983-why-couldnt-jesus-perform-miracles-in-his-hometown. Accessed April 28, 2016.

chapter eleven

Being Led By the Spirit

I have talked to countless Christians who think they have to be "led by the Spirit" in order to share the gospel with someone, or lay hands on a sick person. I believe that this is one of the greatest lies of the enemy. This, along with the lie that you have to have a special gift or calling in order to share the gospel and lay hands on the sick—has limited the Church for much too long! This lie has kept countless people from experiencing healing, deliverance and eternal life. It's time for the church to wake up and be free from this terrible deception.

The fact of the matter is you do not need a special leading by the Holy Spirit in order to share the gospel with someone or lay hands on the sick. Many people who believe that you must be led by the Spirit quote John 5:19 to support their claim. Have you ever noticed that when they quote John 5:19, they do so out of context? Not only do they quote it out of context, but they actually misquote the verse as well!

To truly understand John 5:19 we need to take a look at this verse in context and compare it with some other Scriptures to see what Jesus was really saying. Let's take a look at John 5:1-20:

> *"After this there was a feast of the Jews, and Jesus went up to Jerusalem. Now there is in Jerusalem by the Sheep Gate a pool, which is called in Hebrew, Bethesda,[a] having five porches. In these lay a great multitude of sick people, blind, lame, paralyzed, waiting for the moving of the water. For an angel went down at a certain time into the pool and stirred up the water; then whoever stepped in first, after the stirring of the water, was made well of whatever disease he had. Now a certain man was there who had an infirmity thirty-eight years. When Jesus saw him lying there, and knew that he already had been in that condition a long time, He said to him, "Do you want to be made well?"*
>
> *The sick man answered Him, "Sir, I have no man to put me into the pool when the water is stirred up; but while I am coming, another steps down before me."*

Jesus said to him, "Rise, take up your bed and walk." And immediately the man was made well, took up his bed, and walked.

And that day was the Sabbath. The Jews therefore said to him who was cured, "It is the Sabbath; it is not lawful for you to carry your bed."

He answered them, "He who made me well said to me, 'Take up your bed and walk.'"

Then they asked him, "Who is the Man who said to you, 'Take up your bed and walk'?" But the one who was healed did not know who it was, for Jesus had withdrawn, a multitude being in that place. Afterward Jesus found him in the temple, and said to him, "See, you have been made well. Sin no more, lest a worse thing come upon you."

The man departed and told the Jews that it was Jesus who had made him well.

For this reason the Jews persecuted Jesus, and sought to kill Him, because He had done these things on the Sabbath. But Jesus answered them, "My Father has been working until now, and I have been working."

Therefore the Jews sought all the more to kill Him, because He not only broke the Sabbath, but also said that God was His Father, making

Himself equal with God. **Then Jesus answered and said to them, "Most assuredly, I say to you, the Son can do nothing of Himself, but what He sees the Father do; for whatever He does, the Son also does in like manner.** *For the Father loves the Son, and shows Him all things that He Himself does; and He will show Him greater works than these, that you may marvel."*

Jesus has just finished healing the man at the pool of Bethesda on the Sabbath. The Jews did not like this and looked for Jesus so that they could kill Him. When Jesus said:

"Most assuredly, I say to you, the Son can do nothing of Himself, but what He sees the Father do; for whatever He does, the Son also does in like manner" (John 5:19).

He said this during His confrontation with the Jews. Jesus was not giving the Jews a lesson on evangelism—how to heal the sick or be "led" by the Spirit! Instead, Jesus was saying, "Hey, I have no power to heal the sick on my own. If you have a problem with what I did, take it up with My Father!"

I hear people use John chapter 5 to try and show how Jesus was led by the Spirit all the time. They say things like, "Look, Jesus only did what He saw the Father do and He stepped over a bunch of sick people at the pool of Bethesda just to heal that one man."

However, if you read the story in context you will see that it doesn't say anything about Jesus stepping over a bunch of sick people and just healing the one man. John 5 simply *focuses* on the healing of the individual but never says one way or the other if Jesus healed the other sick people at the pool or not. For all we know He did. But, we don't know for sure so we cannot make assumptions either way, and we certainly can't make a doctrine out of it! Yet many people do. They use this Scripture as a reason to selectively evangelize and say that you must be led by the Spirit in order to share the gospel or pray for a sick person. Personally, if I were to make an assumption about this Scripture I would assume that Jesus also healed others at the pool of Bethesda as well because in the overall context of Scripture that would seem to fit His character.

Acts 10:38 shows us that Jesus did not always have to be led by the Spirit and was not selective when it came to sharing the good news and laying hands on the sick. It says:

> *"...God anointed Jesus of Nazareth with the Holy Spirit and with power, who **went about** doing good and healing **ALL** who were oppressed by the devil, for God was with Him."*

There are two points I want to make from this Scripture. First of all the term "went about" gives us the impression that for the most part Jesus simply walked around from town to town and took every opportunity to minister that presented itself.

Secondly, notice the use of the word "ALL." Jesus did not go about doing good and healing SOME. Jesus did not go about doing good and healing only those he "felt led to heal." Jesus went about doing good and healing "ALL." This is consistent with how Jesus lived His life according to the Gospels. Not once in the Bible do we read about Jesus or the Apostles turning someone away who wanted to be healed because the Holy Spirit was not "leading" them to heal that person.

Jesus was not selective when it came to preaching the good news and healing the sick. Salvation and healing are for everyone! Not just a select few! In the same way, we as Christians should not be selective when it comes to sharing the gospel or laying hands on the sick. When someone is in need, let us be representatives of Jesus, and "do good to ALL" we come in contact with.

Yes, I do believe the Holy Spirit can lead us. But I do not believe in waiting for a leading before I do anything. Too many people don't do anything until they feel "led." Meanwhile, they are passing by countless people who need to hear the gospel or have someone lay hands on them for healing. This to me is not the heart of the Father! God's desire is for EVERYONE to experience salvation (i.e., eternal life, deliverance, freedom and healing). As 2 Corinthians 6:2 says:

"**Now** is the accepted time; behold, **now** is the day of salvation."

Timing is not a good reason for not sharing the gospel, or laying hands on the sick either. You can share the gospel or lay hands on the sick anytime, anywhere! It's for everyone! No leading necessary. In other words, you have freedom to share the gospel and lay hands on the sick wherever you go.

Be "Led" By Love

I have certainly had times when I have been led by the Spirit and He "highlighted" someone to me. But, for the most part, I am led by the two greatest commandments—loving God and loving others. I am led by the "golden rule," which says:

"Therefore, whatever you want men to do to you, do also to them, for this is the Law and the Prophets" (Matthew 7:12).

(Example: If you had cancer wouldn't you want someone to pray for you? Then pray for them!) I believe Jesus was led by compassion all of the time. Rarely do you read that Jesus was "led" to minister to someone because of a vision He saw or a voice He heard. But many times Jesus saw people, had compassion on them, and then healed them.

Years ago, before Curry Blake was in ministry, he asked his pastor (Lester Sumrall, who was discipled by the great apostle of faith, Smith Wigglesworth) two questions that he desperately wanted the answer to. He asked him, "How can I know the will of God?" and, "How can I be sure that I am being led by the Spirit"? His pastor wisely answered, "To know the will of God, read the Bible. To be led by the Spirit, *do* the Bible."[1]

Curry Blake also said, "Most Christians are waiting for a phone call (A special leading) from God, when He has *already* sent us a letter (The Bible.)."[2] In other words, most Christians are waiting for God to give them some sort of "fuzzy feeling," dream/vision or speak to them and tell them specifically what to do before they do anything. However, God has already spoken to us through the Bible, which tells us what to do. Many Christians want the Holy Spirit to guide them like a GPS, giving them step-by-step instructions such as, "Go share the gospel with this person," or "Go lay hands on that person." Yet, the Bible *already* tells us to *go* preach the gospel and lay hands on the sick (Mark 16:15-18)!

Many Christians don't share the gospel or lay hands on the sick unless they are explicitly "led" by the Spirit. In other words they "stay" until they are told to "go." This is the exact opposite of what the disciples did. The disciples "went" until they were told to "stay." Let me give you an example:

"Now when they had gone through Phrygia and the region of Galatia, they were forbidden by the Holy Spirit to preach the word in Asia. After they had come to Mysia, they tried to go into Bithynia, but the Spirit[a] did not permit them. So passing by Mysia, they came down to Troas. And a vision appeared to Paul in the night. A man of Macedonia stood and pleaded with him, saying, "Come over to Macedonia and help us." Now after he had seen the vision, immediately we sought to go to Macedonia, concluding that the Lord had called us to preach the gospel to them" (Acts 16:6-10).

Paul and Silas where simply "going" from town to town preaching the gospel and healing the sick. They were on their way to Asia and Bithynia when the Holy Spirit redirected them to Macedonia. They were obviously not "led by the Spirit" to go into Asia and Bethynia, otherwise the Spirit would not have had to stop them from going to these towns. Paul and Silas were simply obeying the commands of Jesus to "Go into all the world and preach the gospel to every creature." (Mark 16:15) Unlike many believers today they did not have to be led by the Spirit in order to obey what Jesus had *already* commanded them to do! They simply went and as they went they were occasionally led to specific people and places.

I am not against a special leading by the Holy Spirit—I have had many myself. What I am against is the mindset that we cannot share the gospel or lay hands on someone who is sick unless we have a special leading from the Holy Spirit. I get the strong impression from reading the four gospels, and the book of Acts, that Jesus and the Apostles just walked around—town to town—looking for people to minister to. As they went, they were occasionally led to specific people or places. I urge you, don't wait to "go" until you feel a nudge from the Holy Spirit. Just "go," and *as you go*, as the Holy Spirit leads you, then follow.

ENDNOTES

1. http://www.divinerevelations.info/documents/healing/jgl/jgl_ministries.htm. Accessed April 28, 2016.

2. Ibid.

Appendix – A

Step By Step Instructions on How to Minister Healing

* This is just a suggestion. It is not a formula. Only follow these steps if you would like to.

"Before (prayer) test"

1. Ask the person what's wrong? (Example: Back problems.)

2. Ask the person what their pain level is? I use a scale that goes from 0 10. 0 = no pain. 10 – the worst pain they have ever felt. (Example: Pain level 6)

3. Ask the person if there is something they cannot do because of their issue? (Example: They can't bend down to touch there toes.)

4. Ask the person to try to do what they could not do? (Example: They bend down and can only touch their knees.)

By doing this you'll have a baseline and will know the effectiveness of your healing prayers.

5. Minister healing. (Example: "Back be healed.")

   a. Ask the person if you can lay hands on the body part that needs to be healed (Only if it's appropriate). If it's not appropriate or if the person does not feel comfortable with that, it's okay. I have seen many people healed without laying hands on them. I have also seen people healed by praying for them over the phone.

   b. Remember, we are not begging or asking God to heal. We are using the authority He has given us, and commanding healing.

   c. You're words do not need to be specific and your prayer does not need to be long. It can be something as simple as "be healed" or "back be healed."

"After (prayer) test"

6. Ask the person what their pain level is. (Example: 0-10, 0 equals no pain.)

Appendix - A

7. Ask the person to do something they could not do before? (Example: The person bends down and touches their toes)

If the person has no more pain and 100% mobility then your job is done!

8. If the person's condition does not change or it changes, but they are not completely healed, then repeat steps 5-7. You can repeat steps 5-7 as many times as you need to, but be sensitive to the person and any time restraints that they may have. If it's a stranger on the street or at the grocery store, I may only repeat steps 5-7 once or twice. If they are not free of all their pain/symptoms immediately, don't "pull back your faith." Keep believing. I can't tell you how many times I have ministered healing to someone and "nothing" immediate happens. However, a few hours later, the next morning, or a few days later the person tells me that they are 100% healed.

Appendix - B

Resources

This is a list of recommended books, CD's and web sites that have influenced me the most concerning healing, evangelism and the super natural.

CD's

Blake, Curry. *DHT (Divine Healing Technician Training)*. Dallas, TX: John G. Lake Ministries, 1997.

You can purchase this teaching at Curry Blakes website (WWW.JGLM.org) or listen to them for free at: http://www.divinerevelations.info/documents/healing/jgl/jgl_ministries.htm

Website

WWW.JGLM.org (John G. Lake Ministries)

Books

Bosworth, F.F. *Christ the Healer*. Revell, CO: Fleming H., 1994.

Thompson, Steve. *You May All Prophecy*. Fort Mill, SC: MorningStar Publications, Inc., 2005.

Rouse, Ted. *Why Suffering Cannot be God's Will*. Sevierville, TN: Insight Publishing Group, 2003.

Dedmon, Kevin. *The Ultimate Treasure Hunt*. Shippensburg, PA: Destiny Image, 2007.

King, Patricia. *Light Belongs in the Darkness*. Shippensburg, PA: Destiny Image, 2005.

Appendix - C

Sent Ones

To learn more about Sent Ones go to:

www.SentOnes.net

I would love to hear how this book has impacted you. Please feel free to contact me at the email address below.

Also, if you would like to have permission to use part of this book for your small group or bible study, or if you would like to have me speak at your church, special event, or school of ministry, please contact me at:

www.SentOnes11@gmail.com

About the Author

Richie Lewis has had an unquenchable passion to see people enter into a relationship with Jesus Christ since the moment he was saved. Over the years, he has ministered the gospel to thousands of people around the world. In 2011, he became the founder and executive director of Sent Ones Ministries in Harrisburg, Pennsylvania. Richie speaks at churches and ministry schools on healing and evangelism. He leads outreaches and a fellowship that disciples the people they meet during these outreaches. He has a passion to motivate, inspire and equip the body of Christ to reach out beyond the four walls of the Church. Richie and his wife Bethany have been married for ten years and have a seven year old son, Micah.

To order more copies of
Moving Mountains go to:

AMAZON.COM